Religious Education
and the Future

Religious Education and the Future

Edited by

Dermot A. Lane

PAULIST PRESS
New York · Mahawh

 PAULIST PRESS

Published in the United States by
PAULIST PRESS
997 Macarthur Boulevard, Mahwah, NJ 07430

First edition 1986 published by
The Columba Press, Dublin
Design and typography by Bill Bolger
Typesetting by Printset & Design Ltd, Dublin
Printed in Ireland by
Mount Salus Press, Dublin

ISBN 0 8091 2877 2

Library of Congress Catalog Card Number: 86-062152

Contents

Introduction

The successful growth of a child from infancy through adolescence towards some form of adulthood is a matter of fascination and gratitude for parents and close friends. The same can be said about the development of human institutions. One of the people most closely associated with the growth of Mater Dei Institute of Education over the last twenty years was Fr. Patrick Wallace. To him, this collection of essays is offered by way of gratitude, from friends, graduates, students and staff.

From 1969 to 1982 Fr. Wallace served as Director of Studies in Mater Dei Institute of Education. During that time he laid firm foundations for the development of the Institute as a College of Education specialising in the academic and professional formation of Religious Educators for post-primary schools in Ireland. At the same time he also set out to establish the nature and identity of Religious Education within the Irish context as a third level discipline in itself with its own particular dynamic.

Of course, many others were also closely involved in the growing up of Mater Dei Institute. Mention must be made of the foundation of the Institute in 1966 by the former Archisbishop of Dublin, the late John Charles McQuaid. What was insightfully set in motion by Archbishop McQuaid was energetically expanded by the late Archbishop Dermot Ryan from 1972 to 1984. Since then, the present Archbishop of Dublin, Dr. Kevin McNamara, has continued the tradition of his predecessors and has already promoted its development. Brief reference must also be made to the dedicated work of Bishop Joseph A. Carroll, Mother Mary Jordana, O.P., Bishop Dermot O'Mahony, Bishop James Kavanagh, and the Rev. Professor Michael Nolan. It will be the task of others to elaborate more explicitly the painstaking work of these and others. For the moment the focus is on the lasting contribution of Fr. Wallace.

It would be unwise to try to capture in an introduction of this kind all the qualities that Fr. Wallace brought to bear on the life and work of Mater Dei Institute. Having had the privilege of working closely with him for twelve years one thinks immediately of his natural kindness and courtesy to people at all times. With students, he always had a sympathetic ear and an encouraging word. In relation to staff, he enabled the best within them to emerge and to flourish. As a Religious Educator, he used the medium of poetry and story, leaving his audience the freedom to unpack and to interpret. When it came to administration, he had an irrepressible optimism that enabled him to see in the dark when everyone else had almost given up hope.

In the summer of 1982 Fr. Wallace was appointed Parish Priest of Celbridge in the diocese of Dublin. At that time, it was the spontaneous reaction of all concerned that his contribution to the life of Mater Dei and the work of Religious Education should be honoured in some significant way. Out of that consensus grew the idea of holding a series of public lectures in the Institute in honour of Fr. Wallace with a view to eventual publication. These lectures took place between 1983 and 1986 and are now presented in the form of a *Festschrift* to Fr. Wallace and to the wider reading public.

The lectures do not appear in this symposium in the particular order in which they were originally presented. Instead, they have been re-arranged with a view to providing some overall coherence and sequence to their publication in book form.

Part One provides three quite different progress reports on the state of Religious Education in different countries. Andreas Baur, of Augsburg, outlines what has been happening concerning Religious Instruction in German schools and indicates his belief in the desirability of some form of catechism as a guide. He notes in particular the need for Religious Instruction in schools to be complemented by catechesis in parishes. Didier Piveteau, from Paris, reviews historically the social and cultural changes that have taken place in recent times and shows how these have affected the role of Religious Education in terms of initiation and schooling. Michael Wrenn, from New York, gives his understanding of what has been going on in the United States over the last twenty years in catechetics. He pays particular attention to the impact of the *General Catechetical Directory* on Religious Education and outlines certain proposals for the future of Religious Education.

Part Two takes up some of the issues raised in Part one. Berard L. Marthaler, from the Catholic University of America in Washington D.C., who is the *Doktorvater* of Fr. Wallace, gives us a history of the catechisms and its use as an instrument of catechesis in the Church. He weighs up the pros and cons of the present discussion surrounding the call issued at the Extraordinary Synod in Rome of 1985 for a catechism or a compendium of Catholic doctrine. Gabriel Moran analyses the meaning of development implicit in much of moral and religious education. He expresses reservations about the idea of development as some kind of growth without restriction and supports his case by appealing to feminism, ecology, spirituality and religion. Michael Warren, of New York, examines the relationship between catechesis and pastoral ministry. He shows how evangelisation leads to catechesis and catechesis gives rise to worship. He also discusses the place of Religious Education as distinct from catechesis in schools.

Part Three proposes tentative responses to some of the problems facing Religious Education today. Una O'Neill, from Dublin and a former student of Fr. Wallace, calls for the recovery of the symbolic imagination as a safeguard against the functionalist approach that has become so common today and as a corrective to a purely conceptualist understanding of the content of faith. Donal Murray confronts the catechetical problem of finding a language that takes account of the socio-cultural changes of the world we live in and yet at the same time expresses the one faith of the Christian tradition. He suggests that the language of catechesis should be a complete language and a language shared by the whole Church made up of school, home and parish. Kevin Nichols, of England, looks at classical education and contempory liberation-movements as complementary rather than in opposition. He outlines how these two approaches have something to offer to each other in the realm of Religious Education. A similar concern is taken up by Dermot Lane who sees the challenge facing Religious Education as one of integrating the universal struggle for justice with the vision of the gospel. One way forward is to unite the Christian tradition and shared action for justice in a mutually enriching correlation. Out of this will come a new way of learning in Religious Education that could begin to unite the theory and practice of Christian faith.

The questions faced in this collection of essays do not admit of easy, ready-made answers. An essential ingredient in the enterprise of Religious Education is learning to be secure with living questions. In Religious Education keeping the question alive is as important as knowing the answer. It was this kind of philosophy that inspired and sustained so much of Fr. Wallace's work in the field of Religious Education. For his lasting contribution to Mater Dei Institute and the work of Religious Education we are all in his debt.

In conclusion, a word of thanks must be recorded to all the friends, graduates, students and staff of Mater Dei who sponsored the foundation of this series of public lectures in honour of Fr. Wallace. Appreciation also must be extended for the gracious hospitality of Clonliffe College offered to our guest speakers in the person of

Monsignor John J. Greehy, former President of the Seminary and long-time member of the academic staff of Mater Dei Institute, and his successor Monsignor Brendan Houlihan. Lastly, I wish to thank all the staff, academic and administrative, of Mater Dei Institute who contributed so much to the planning and organisation of these public lectures. Among them, I must single out Sr. Marcellina O'Sullivan who was always there to help, way beyond the call of duty, in season and out of season. Without this generous spirit of co-operation from so many people associated with Mater Dei, the mounting of this series of public lectures in honour of Fr. Wallace and their publication as a *Festschrift* would not have been possible.

Dermot A. Lane,
June, 1986.

PART ONE

Progress Reports on the State of Religious Education

Teaching Religion in Germany : An Historical Overview

Andreas Baur

In St. Gallen, in Switzerland last summer, I saw in its ancient monastery, the little bell which in the 7th century the Irish monk, St. Gall, used to ring to call people to come and listen to the Good News of the Gospels. Gall was one of the many Irish monks who came as missionaries to what are the German-speaking countries of today. The oldest church in my own native city, Augsburg in Bavaria, is consecrated to St. Gall. So the catechetical link between Ireland and Germany dates back many centuries. It is true that the christian mission in Germany began with the Romans and flourished under the Anglo-Saxons. St. Boniface forged firm links with the Papacy and Rome, but the seed sown by Gall, the Irish monk, is remembered and acknowledged down the centuries.

In this paper, I wish to give a picture of the catechetical situation in Germany today. I want to show how the catechetical enterprise evolved in our country, and the problems we foresee in the future. I must first of all emphasise three points:

1. School in Germany is essentially an institution of the State. There are independent Catholic schools, but they are only a minority.
2. The shortage of priests in Germany is acute both for school and parish ministry. Lay persons are increasingly employed as religious instruction teachers.
3. More and more, parish catechesis supplements religious instruction in the schools. Members of the parish are encouraged to undertake this work.

Catholicism in Germany : A Backward Glance

Nearly five hundred years ago the Reformation swept through Germany. After the Thirty Years' War (1618-1648) the German people were split into Catholics and Protestants. The country itself was divided into Catholic and Protestant regions.

The Second Reich began in 1871. Under this regime, Catholics were suspected of ultramontanism, i.e. "belonging to those beyond the mountains", and it was Rome that was beyond the mountains. Until

11

the first world war Catholics were treated as second class citizens. As a result of concordats with the individual federal states of Germany, the Church secured the right of a "presence" in the schools. Religious instruction and education were guaranteed recognition in the school curriculum: *(ordentliches Lehrfach)*. The *Reichskonkordat* between Germany and the Vatican in 1933 again acknowledged the importance of religious education in the schools, but Hitler did not really intend to respect the rights of the Church.

After the break-down of the Hitler regime, it was found that the Church was one of the few institutions that had survived almost intact. But new post-war problems soon arose. Millions of refugees from East-German regions occupied by the Soviet Union, Poland and Czechoslovakia, moved from east to west. The movement of these millions made much more evident the pluralism of religious commitment in Germany. Catholics formed only a small minority in the east of the country. In the west the ratio of Catholics and Protestants is now about 50%. In the very difficult post-war years, there grew up a new collaboration between Catholics and Protestants; but this collaboration was perhaps more on political than religious grounds.

In this present age, it is very significant that Germany is a federal republic, as each individual state has freedom in school affairs. This means though, that school is an institution of the State and that there is no uniformity, particularly in the religious education system. Independent Catholic schools are run by religious orders and are generally limited to grammar schools *(Gymnasium und Realschule)*. The *Reichskonkordat* of 1933 is still in force. Also, the German constitution decrees that in West Germany religious instruction is recognised as a regular school subject *(ordentliches Lehrfach)*. The Church enjoys great freedom in schools, in parishes, in the mass media. One could therefore wonder, "What more do you want?"

Catechetical orientations in Germany during the last decades (1950 — 1980)
In the last centuries, German Catechesis was limited almost exclusively to children in school. Since the days of St. Peter Canisius the Catechism was the primary catechetical textbook. It was supplemented by Bible history. Some biblical stories were used:

a.   to provide the children with a knowledge of the facts of divine revelation,
b.   to encourage a love of the Bible,
c.   to set before the young, moral examples of Christian commitment.

This type of school catechesis was supplemented in the parishes by Sunday school religious instruction. *(Christenlehre)*.

The Catechism of 1955

The German Catechism of 1955 was welcomed in every diocese of Germany and in many other European countries. It was a departure from the mere doctrinal question-and-answer approach of the Canisius Catechism. In outline, it followed the doctrinal mysteries of the Credo and the linear recountal of God's saving deeds in human history, as crystallized in the Scriptures. The Green Catechism, as it was called in Germany, consisted of 136 lessons. The lessons were structured on a uniform plan:
1. A scriptural text.
2. An instruction or teaching.
3. Questions for reflection on the text.
4. Sentences for memorizing.
5. Rules for living.
6. Biblical words, maxims, exercises.

There were pictorial illustrations that helped to make the biblical history concrete and palpable. The response to this book from priests and teachers was very positive. It was scripture-rooted, liturgy-centred and evoked a prayer response. Though didactically excellent, it was soon discovered that it was a book for believers, for people already initiated in the faith. It did not seem to touch the lives of the indifferent or the unbelieving. Less than ten years after its publication, Vatican Council II was convened. With the new insights of Vatican II, many catechetical experiments were tried, some good and others not so good. It became clear that the lessons of the German Catechism were out of touch with the life situation of the Church and no longer met the real needs of pupils. Many Catechists still regret that the Green Catechism was popular for only ten years.

Framework for Instruction in Faith 1967

In 1967, a new plan for religious instruction was drawn up *(Rahmenplan)*. This Plan was the second outstanding achievement for religious instruction in Germany. Its authors saw distinctly that religious instruction in the schools was isolated from the adult christian community in the parish. The Plan tried to find bridges between the school and parish life and, within the school itself, the Plan hoped to forge links between religious instruction and other educational disciplines. The documents of Vatican II influenced the orientations of the Plan. In its introduction the Plan highlights the following points made at the Council:
a. The Christian believer no longer lives in a Christian milieu.
b. Our world is in a period of rapid change where traditions are openly questioned.

c. The Church must identify a hierarchy of fundamental truths.

The *Framework for Instruction in Faith* did not last very long, but basically, it was an excellent document. It centred on:
    The doctrine of the Church.
    The persons addressed.
    The Catechetical ministry.

In structure it gave primary place to Scripture and placed the memorization of the catechism as secondary to the biblical text. Religious instruction was meant to flow over into christian living and liturgical celebration. The ground plan of the instruction would be: Bible/Catechism/Liturgy/Christian life.
The aims of the Plan were too comprehensive for school-life only. Also, the task of seeing real life in the light of Scripture proved daunting. Religious experts in Germany began to distinguish between the concept of religious education in school and catechesis in the parishes. In 1969-70 the Conference of German Bishops was concerned with critical developments in schools, parishes and in society as a whole, and the impact of these developments on religious education. The Common Synod of German dioceses discussed the situation and formulated guidelines in an important paper entitled, "Religious Instruction in the School". The main problems outlined in the paper were:
    the plurality of ideologies in society,
    religious indifference,
    the tension between Catechesis for believers and instruction for unbelievers or the indifferent,
    the secularization of society,
    scientific and materialistic advances,
    the impact of mass media, especially on youth,

The fundamental questions posed by the paper were:
1. What does faith mean in our time and society, in a world of prosperity, of progress, of apparently unlimited possibilities?
2. Is faith, Christian faith, a great and good force now and for the future?
3. How can faith be made to appear as light, as liberation, as a help to find meaning in human existence?

Public discussion about and against religious education in schools became louder. Withdrawal from instruction became more and more frequent. Young people were rebellious and teachers of religion faced a daunting task. It became very clear that religious instruction in the

14

schools would have meaning for life only if all God's people in the Church *initiated* their young children into christian faith in a family which believed and prayed, in a living parish community where the majority of people worshipped together and celebrated the liturgical feasts of the Church. These insights led catechists to distinguish between religious instruction in school and christian initiation in parishes.

New Curriculum
New problems in religious education needed new orientations. The German Catechetical Union and religion teachers cried out for a new curriculum, which would instil vigour into the catechetical enterprise in the eyes of students and of the larger public. This new word from Latin, curriculum, replaced by the old German word "*Lehrplan*". It symbolized more than an outline of content to be taught. Its underlying goal was to lead young people to maturity of faith in self-deliberation and Christian conduct. To implement this aim the curriculum outlined means, themes, topics, methods. A flood of catechetical literature was the result and this in turn gave rise to the *Zielfelderplan* which is in force in many parts of Germany, though not in Bavaria.

The Field Plan for Catechesis : The Zielfelderplan
This was a curriculum suggesting anthropological and religious approaches. It saw human experience as the locus for the living out of biblical faith and Church doctrine. The *Zielfelderplan* was comprehensive and difficult. It led to the publication of many aid-books for teachers and students. It is under revision at the present time. Many readers of the Plan over-emphasized the anthropological, experiential starting point and neglected the illuminating religious and doctrinal dimension of christian living. Doctrines proposed for belief had an important place in the Plan but were often treated as problems for discussion only, instead of proclamations by the Church proposed for personal life. The implementation of the Plan depended much on the initiatives, expertise, faith-convictions and lifestyles of the teachers. Many people attacked the Plan because the old securities of a body of memorized knowledge were lost. Pupils could no longer recite the Our Father, The Ten Commandments, the Credo. But these consequences, I think, were more the result of the secularized spirit which influenced families and societal milieu.

The Specific Aims of Catechesis (Zielspektrum)
The impasse which resulted from the *Zielfelderplan* urged the German Bishops to declare officially the aims of religious instruction in schools.

These aims were given in the *Zielspektrum*. Briefly these aims embrace the following points concerning religious instruction:

> Religious instruction evokes the question of God, the interpretation of the world, the meaning and value of human existence, the responsibility of human acts. It enables one to find answers to these questions in the divine self-revelation of God and the faith of the Church.

> Religious instruction initiates one into the personal response of faith and enables one to find a rational foothold for faith.

> Religious instruction examines the beliefs of other denominations, religions and ideologies. It aims to create understanding of other people's religious convictions.

> Religious instruction motivates one to live a committed christian life in church and in society.

This significant directive of the German Bishops became the basis for the decisions on religious instruction of the Synod of 1974.

The *General Catechetical Directory* from Rome was published in 1971. Because of internal curriculum problems in Germany the General Directory made little impact on catechesis in Germany. It was some years later before a German translation of the Directory appeared.

In contrast, it was very different with *Catechesi Tradendae*. This important document was translated immediately into German, and was followed by a commentary by Adolf Exeler, the late German scholar in religious education. To implement the directives of *Catechesi Tradendae* in the German situation was a much more daunting task than merely writing a German version. The reasons for this difficulty could be seen as the following:

1. The Universal Church does not distinguish so much between religious instruction in schools and catechesis in parishes.
2. The guidelines of the Directory were aimed specifically at Catholic schools, but in Germany the schools were run by the State in a very secularized society.
3. Both the General Directory and *Catechesi Tradendae* emphasised systematic theological instruction on a clearly chosen hierarchy of truths. The German curriculum took as its starting point anthropological approaches to life and human experience.

The Synod of Wurtbürg (1971 — 1975)

The Synod of Wurtbürg was convened to adapt the insights of Vatican Council II to the German situation. Representatives from all dioceses included laymen and women as well as bishops. Many important questions were on the agenda but only the catechetical question concerns us in this paper.

The synod justified the teaching of religious instruction in state-run schools under three headings:

1. An argument from cultural tradition. Young people in school must be made acquainted with the traditions of their people.
2. The anthropological argument. Education in school must enable students to answer questions concerning the meaning, purpose and destiny of human existence.
3. The social argument. Education in school must enable students to face, in a positive way, the challenges of our time and our world.

These arguments were impressively elaborated and supported by theological insights. This forged a theological and educational foundation for maintaining religious instruction as "a necessary school subject".

The *Zielspektrum* of our Bishops and the Synod of Wurtbürg provided guidelines for the religious text-books which have appeared in Germany in the last decades. The variety of catechetical approaches in these text-books held an inherent danger. Both catechists and pupils could side-track into never-ending discussion on problem areas in life and society without ever attaining a clear grasp of the systematic structure of the hierarchy of truths about God, human existence, and this world. In these last years the main concern of religious educators in Germany is to put major emphasis on central themes of Christian faith. It was the Synod of Wurtbürg which alerted us to the vital importance of this catechetical task.

The second great merit of the Wurtbürg Synod was its strong demand for Parish Catechesis to complement and support religious instruction in schools. In a paper entitled "The Catechetical Activities of the Church" (1973) the Synod set out proposals for the initiation and practice of Parish Catechesis.

1. Parish Catechesis should be directed to people of all ages, but in a particular way to adults: to the older generation, to parents, to the lapsed and the unbelieving, to the sick and the dying, to prisoners, to the poor and to professionals.
2. The Synod refused to acknowledge any alternative between religious instruction in school and parish catechesis. One presupposes and complements the other. They are different phases of one ministry. They may be compared to the two focal points of an ellipse. They vary in approach, in concern for the persons addressed, but the ideal would be that of a close collaboration between school and parish.
3. Because of the scarcity of priests, Wurtbürg foresees the

involvement of lay persons in the catechetical ministry. Ideally, every member of the parish should use his talents for the benefit of the community as a whole.

4. The goals of parish catechesis would emphasize as primary: concientization of beliefs, christian commitment to Church and world, awareness of the spiritual potential of human existence.

At present in Germany, parish catechesis seems to go step by step with the liturgical celebration of the Sacraments of Holy Communion and Confirmation. This is good, but only a first stage. The possibilities of adult religious education are manifold and would open avenues of real christian commitment to many men and women who would be ready to serve the People of God at parish level.

Some Remarks on Religious Instruction in Germany Today

Allow me to conclude with a few observations on the current situation concerning religious instruction in Germany.

Religious instruction in schools is a subject with examinations and grades (marks) up to the last classes of grammar school, including final examinations.

Most religion teachers in primary schools and in grammar schools are well-trained lay persons. These teachers are trained in universities and employed by the State. The Church invests them with a canonical mission *(Missio Canonica)* which they need to be allowed by the State to teach. The Church trains priests and lay persons in its own academies and colleges. These catechists are paid by the Church.

Religious instruction is a regular school subject, but it is possible to opt out on ethical grounds. In many federal states of Germany, it is compulsory for those who opt out of religious instruction in school to attend a school course in ethics. Since this course was made compulsory the number who opt out of religion classes has dropped considerably.

Need for a Handbook for Adults

Contemplata aliis tradere; i.e. what you have meditated and contemplated, teach to others. But what is the adult to meditate and to contemplate? There is a proliferation of catechetical textbooks, a variety of approaches to the catechetical task, a pluralism in theology which is baffling for the uninitiated, an encroaching secularism which threatens all religious commitment. How can Christian Faith be seen to be relevant and convincing? How can the faith of the Church be brought into a good correlation with the experiences of life today? What is the foundational substance of our faith? How can essentials be emphasised and non-essentials laid aside? Where can we find a concise canon of truth to be believed and values to be lived? Is the catechist left alone with the predicament of reading his human experience and the experience of others in the light of God's divine self-disclosure to humanity?

I personally believe that neither religious instruction nor parish catechesis will succeed without a handbook or a kind of catechism for adults. It ought to be a book that will lead to meditative insight into the mystery of God, the wonder of human existence and the biblical history of God's saving deed in Jesus Christ. German Protestants have a book of this kind. I am happy to hear that a book I have written with some friends, entitled *The Message of the Faith*, helps catechists to do their work better.[1] Since the appearance of that book, the German Association of Catechists have published a Catechism called *Outline of the Faith*.[2] However, there is scarcely any room in schools for a Catechism beside the handsomely illustrated texts books and school Bibles.

By far the most important event of 1985 has been the publication by the Catholic Bishops' Conference of an adult catechism, written mainly by Professor Walter Kasper of Tubingen bearing the title *A Catholic Adult Catechism : the Church's Profession of Faith*.[3] This text has been published simultaneously by seven publishers in Germany. The book is intended for many different kinds of audiences, is theologically demanding, and will certainly be useful in schools. It is particularly important for parish Catechists. It is clear, of course, that the simple reader will be overtaxed by it. I am, therefore, all the more pleased to have been able to publish a "small" Catechism for families and children: *My Book of Faith — On the Way with God*.[4] This Catechism is richly illustrated and has been well received. I hope it reaches people "at the grassroots" and that it helps families to get involved in religious dialogue and prayer together.

The task of catechesis is a tremendous challenge. It cannot be more efficient than the christian faith out of which it springs and which it aspires to bring to maturity in Christ.

Empowered by God we can succeed. Everyday, let up pray: *Veni, Sancte Spiritus*.

1. A. Baur und W. Plöger, *Botschatt des Glaubens*, : L. Auer. Donauwörth, 1978.
2. *Graudris des Glaubens*, Kösel-Verlag, München, 1984.
3. *Katholischer Erwachsenenkatechismus Das Glaubensbekenntnis Der Kirch*, Verlag Butzon Und Bercker, 1985.
4. A. Baur, J. Bongers, W. Plöger, *Mein Glaubensbuch. Auf dem Weg mit Gott*, Verlot, L. Auer, Donauwörth, 1986.

School, Society and Catechetics

Didier Piveteau

Introduction

In the month of January 1983, Cardinal Ratzinger, lecturing from the pulpit of Notre Dame in Paris warned the Church in France about the tendencies at work in the field of French Catechetics. He deemed there was not sufficient emphasis on dogmas, that it was too narrowly existential and encouraged the French bishops to remedy the situation. Lately, (February, 1985) just a few months ago, the same Cardinal explicitly asked the French bishops to put an end to the proliferation of text books and asked for the publication of a unified text that would be the basis for all educational variations sought by the various dioceses.

This is, I think, symbolic of the problem that faces Religious Education in many countries. Some claim that Religious Education has gone astray over the last twenty years and point to the lack of Religious Knowledge common among contemporary youngsters. Others judge that a neo-insistance on doctrine is a regression to a pre-conciliar practice, a journey back to the past....

Actually, the issue is much more important than just knowing what should be taught to children. At heart it is first of all a misunderstanding between most theologians and those whom we call pastors or educators in the Church. Even deeper it reveals opposite views developed after the Council on such issues as Revelation, the nature and significance of Christ, the nature of the Church. In other words, Religious Education is the projection of all the problems and questions that are raised in Christianity today. This is why it is such a fascinating subject to analyse and study.

I suggest that we examine the two traditional dimensions of education and the particular position that our parents were in, throughout the 19th century down to the end of the second world war. Then we shall be in a better position to understand what has befallen us during the last twenty-five years. Finally we will venture to formulate what can be done in the present situation that constitutes our *Hodie*.

Throughout space (ethnology) and time (history) human societies have always had recourse to either initiation or to schooling to transmit behaviours and values to the oncoming generations. Both ways of educating the young are legitimate and efficient but the field of their efficiency is different.[1]

Initiation is a *global* process of education. It takes place when society as a whole functions like a matrix giving birth not to a carnal body, but to a corporate mind and heart. The conditions for an easy and sound functioning of the initiation process are that the given society be *stable* and unanimous. The global process means that the educational process is not limited to a specific time, in a specific place. It is not entrusted to a specific body of educators and it is geared to all the young in general with no regards to age, sometimes not even to sex.

Such an education of course is not highly cognitive in nature and it is not at all critical. Society cannot teach an attitude which might cause its ruin. It plays with full efficiency when it is applied to transmitting not knowledge or concepts, but stories, traditions, behaviours and the values that are the cement of the given society.

We might have a tendency to consider that initiation is a process that may still be used in backward tribes, but that our society has done away with it. Nothing could be more erroneous. It is still the only method used for introducing infants to the control of their mother tongue. Up to very recently this was also the method used by women to teach young girls cooking and child-care, by men to teach boys fishing and hunting and by society at large to teach both boys and girls the mystery of sex.

Quite opposite is the nature of schooling which is a *specialised*, intentional process of education. It is specialised in as much as it takes place at certain times of the day, certain days of the week; it is dispensed in special places, by a body of teachers who are paid by society to fulfil a function that society can no longer fulfil. Such schooling is specialised finally in its clientele: children eight years old being separated from eleven years old, bright children being separated from children less alert and so on.

Schooling is particularly well adapted to the transmission of cognitive contents: facts, concepts, relationships, laws, theories etc.... It teaches a critical attitude *vis à vis* what is lived spontaneously and given by society and therefore it is a tool perfectly adapted for research and

1.   Cf. John H. Westerhoff and Gwen Kennedy Nevill, *Generation to Generation*, Pilgrim Press, 1974.

progress. In short it is an excellent means of transmitting and building both knowledge and know-how.

But as a consequence it is not fitted at all to transmit values. Values need to be *nurtured*. Values are not essentially cognitive in nature: they belong more to the kingdom of the heart.

Now our lack of solid historical knowledge has prevented us from seeing how Religious Education fits with the two processes. Our recent past (19th century and first half of the 20th century) has been a unique moment in the relationship of the two ways of education. That period has known at the same time and in a beautiful combination both initiation and schooling. Our societies were still sufficiently *unanimous* and *self-enclosed*, the rhythm of change was such that it did not endanger stability so that those societies functioned as matrices giving birth to new generations acknowledging the same values and traditions as the generations that had preceded them. At the same time schooling was largely developed and allowed an intellectual understanding of the elements of religion, a capacity for verbal explanation. Religious Education as a consequence bore fruit. On the whole the four or five generations that lived during that period exhibited a fair knowledge of the rudiments of christianity (probably a better knowledge than any other generation in the history of the Church) and at the same time a willingness to participate in the rites and commitments of the Church.

What was not known was: to which process of education could these fruits be attributed. Gradually the importance of initiation was forgotten about and the happy results of Religious Education were attributed to schooling, namely the intentional, long-lasting instruction called Catechetics. This was an error due to the fact that at that time schooling assumed an ever-increasing importance in the general field of education. It was an error on two stands:

First it tended to obliviate the traditional importance of initiation in the history of christianity. Let us remember that three of our sacraments are precisely called *Sacraments of Initiation*. Let us bear in mind that the Church has always held that "Faith seeks understanding" (*Fides querens intellectum*) but never that knowledge produces faith because faith is a gift from above. And let us recall finally that faith had been transmitted in the Church for fifteen centuries without the help of a formal generalised schooling of children. It was Luther, who for the first time thought of teaching children a formal theological summary of the Creed.

Secondly, this insistence on schooling blurred the mechanism through which the wonderful results of the transmission of faith in the 19th century were obtained. Actually it worked that way. Through family life, parish participation, cultural environment, children were initiated into the values of christianity. And then catechetics (schooling) could make *explicit*, that is, clothe in words, what the children already lived *implicitly*. Such an education was at the same time existential and cognitive. Of course, such an education, in spite of its excellence had its necessary limitations. The Word of God was patterned according to the type of surrounding society, that is, it was pyramidal, highly hierarchical, faith was more gregarious than really personal and the faithful remained children of the Church, cherishing obedience and docility more than creativity and role-taking.

Such was the situation until the end of the fifties. Many people thought it had been the situation throughout the history of the Church, whereas it has been in operation for little more than a hundred and twenty years.

The Shock of the Last Twenty-Five Years

Suddenly at the turn of the sixties the situation began to change drastically. Those changes may be attributed to three main causes.

The growth of technology that has speeded up the course of history. Formerly it took nearly one century to go from one technique to an entirely different one (cf. the styles of castles or cathedrals). Nowadays it takes less than five years to go from one generation of computer or radar to another. The result is that little by little, people, especially the young who have had no other previous experience, lose the sense of duration, continuity and develop instead a now-consciousness (notice the contemporary use of the word "instant": instant coffee; instant relief; instant washing; instant soup etc....) Society is no longer stable, but is rocked on the waves of change. Now, stability as we remember, was one condition for initiation to take place.[2]

People reacted differently to this challenge of constant and forced change. Some do resist and try to find shelters against novelty. Some are enthusiastic and would like changes to be more radical, more encompassing. This is to say that little by little the unanimity of society becomes fractured and we live now in a pluralistic society, harbouring various tendencies with opposite values, diversified behaviours and distinct expectations. Now again unanimity is one of the conditions necessary for initiation being made possible.

Schooling has developed over the stage it had reached in the 19th century. By the end of that century, in a country like France only 5% of the population were attending secondary school. The rest were confined to primary education. Now in 1985, more than 75% benefit

2. Cf. Alvin Toffler, *Future Shock*, New York, Random House, 1980.

from getting a high school education. The importance of that evolution cannot be underestimated. For the difference is immense between primary and secondary education. In primary education the student *memorises* facts and data; he experiences rote learning and the curriculum is mostly *product-centred*. In secondary education the curriculum is *process-centred;* the student takes a *critical, personal* view of the data he comes in contact with. The result is that little by little, there is a growing development of individualism, in which everyone becomes the tape and measure of his own set of values, not accepting them any more from authority or tradition. This has even consequences on the use of language. Traditionally language has three usages: it can be used for *repetition;* it can be used for the *expression* of self and finally it can be used for *communication*. A unanimous, stable society that has only primary schools such as was the case in the 19th century favours the repetitive discourse. Whereas a pluralistic, unstable, individualistic society favours the language of expression (note the frequent use of this word in contemporary talk: expressive dancing; bodily expression; expressive painting etc.....).

Finally the modern means of communication, especially television, entirely disrupts the sanctuaries where initiation took place. Family life and neighbourhood have become distant influences on the growth of children whereas the modern means of communication are preventing these natural communities from functioning as matrices to initiate the younger generation.

The consequence of these changes is that initiation of any kind has become quasi impossible in contemporary society. Education, whether it be secular or religious, walks on one leg only: namely schooling. Secular education did not care at first; after all, as has been seen, schooling is a wonderful tool for progress and research, for competition and the development of an elite, and these have been the goals of western society for the last three decades. Only recently did some people ask themselves whether there can be any society at all without some kind of tradition, and without some initiation into a common set of values.

The Church, who should have known better, first followed the general tendencies and based her action on two false assumptions. The first prompted the Church to believe that if the process of initiation was made difficult through the fractures of society, the looseness of family rearing, the gradual disappearance of a christian environment, the danger, after all was not that great and could be balanced by an emphasis on schooling and formal Religious instruction. Hence the fantastic development, unprecedented before, both quantitative and qualitative of courses for children and for adolescents, the insistance

24

on training catechists, the publishing of excellent and attractive text-books and the rest. The second false assumption led Religious Education to believe that if initiation became difficult for the reasons cited above, they could achieve some equivalent of initiation by making catechetics *less cognitive* and *more existential*.[3] This is a paradox of the situation that has been developing all those years: The Church has developed tremendously the schooling approach to Religious Education (formal catechetics) but has used the structure to try to foster initiation, a task for which it has never been meant.

In the light of these considerations a number of recent researches and practices, that might appear to have been adopted at random, take their meaning. Following here again the general tendencies of schools, catechetics, in its wish to constitute an initiating environment has become child-centred. Three schools of thought have brought the help of their theories and practices to well-meaning religious educators, and their influence can be traced throughout all the lectures, articles, and text-books that have been the basis of the catechetical movement for the past thirty years. One is Piaget and his disciple Kohlberg, who have advocated the existence of phases in the child's development and who have excluded the possibility of abstract thinking before the age of ten approximately. A second one is Rogers, whose practice is at the origin of the non-directive approach, and who insisted on the fact that there is an affective dimension to learning while defining learning at the same time as the mere unfolding of the innate. And finally people like Lewin or Bion who evidenced the small group influence on individual learning and who innovated in recommending learning situations in small groups and free intercommunications.

Two catechists have had a traceable influence at least until the mid-seventies and over all Western Europe and the United States in translating these general theories of learning and education into the Christian field. One was the Belgian Jesuit, Van Caster, who advocated the dynamics of all catechetical presentation as progressive along three steps. The gospel message was to be presented as being a fulfilment of human values, as transcending, calling beyond those human values and finally as being sometimes in opposition to those sames values. The other one was the French Oblate, Pierre Babin, who appeared to be an excellent interpreter of secular theories into catechetical practices.[4]

3. Cf. On all those aspects of faith see G. Rummery and D. Lundy, *Growing into Faith*, Darton, Longman and Todd, London, 1980.
4. Marcel Van Caster, *Experiential Catechetics*, 1969; P. Babin, *Crisis of Faith*, New York: Herder and Herder, 1963, T. Groome, *Christian Religious Education*, New York: Harper and Row, 1981.

The general impression that one gets after all those years of tremendous effort is an ambiguous one. On the one hand, one cannot help admiring the quality and sophistication that catechetics (the schooling approach) has reached. In all countries, there is not one single school system that has reached the quality of the various catechetical courses. And on the other hand one cannot help observing that it is of no avail. All those efforts are nearly in vain, for the efficiency is minimal indeed. Never have children and teenagers been so confused in their understanding of christianity and so erratic in their commitment. They do not master the meaning of words, they are ignorant of the *Mirabilia Dei*, as narrated in the Bible and in the Liturgy, and they have only fleeting motivations to participate in any form of church life.

Perhaps it was impossible to do otherwise during that period of turmoil. We cannot be blamed for the poor results obtained. But we sure can blame ourselves for displaying so little independent thinking. The objectives of the Church, the nature of christianity are different from the objectives of this secular society and from the nature of this world. Society can do, perhaps, without an initiating process and even that is not sure. But christianity cannot dispense from that form of transmission. The reason for this is that christianity is *life* and not *theories*;, christianity deals with *values* not with *words* and *opinions*; Christianity needs transmission through *human communities* and not through *books*.

A world can be conceived where Christianity would be alive and operative without any book existing. The same world cannot be thought of where there would be as many books as may be imagined but where there would be no human communities.

It would have been important therefore in the sixties to think more about ways to foster initiation through alternatives to parishes in terms of small communities, than to try to build the best schooling approach possible. It has not been done, or too late and on a small scale. We will have to pay the price of our lack of vigilance for at least one generation; and we must now think of what can be done in the years to come.

And Now
It must seem obvious by now that some of the following two orientations can be looked upon as possible solutions for the future.
   — It is in vain that we may hope to secure the transmission of Christianity by still more efforts and investments on the schooling approach of education, namely catechetics.

— It is also in vain that we try to recapture the situation of the past, when Christianity was co-extensive with society and when culture at large was predominantly Christian.

One of those solutions belongs decidedly to the past, while the other has proved to be notably insufficient.

In the face of the present state of affairs we must be ready to face the facts that at least for one generation, education of the faith will have mostly to deal with adults and not with children. Our generation has failed in great part in awakening the young to Christian values, in motivating them to be personally committed to the life of the Church. We will have to wait for them to reach adult age when new challenges will invite them to give meaning to their lives; getting married; taking the decision to have children; making an option for a particular kind of life-style (self-centred, dedication, service) through their career choice.

One cannot do away with the possibility that the present situation will last over one generation. Several indications seem to point out that this could be the case for society at large, which would be in constant change, oblivious of any tradition, permanently fractured into pluralism, unable to gather people on secure territory with a minimum of unanimity and common values. It would be a premier in the history of humanity because never before have there been such types of society. One could well imagine then, that Christianity in such a case would play a therapeutic role, as has often been the case in the past, by offering people a kind of anchorage where initiation could still be possible. If this is not done, then we will have a new concept of Christianity, a new concept of the Church. It will not be a visible people, but a dilution of the Gospel into the world, somewhat like the leaven in the dough. It is not up to us to foster such a concept so foreign to the whole tradition of the Church and so foreign also to the nature of man, since this nature is not defined *a priori* by intellectuals.

To contribute to the advent of a world where Christianity could use the two traditional approaches to education, namely initiation and schooling, without returning to the past is our task. Three main orientations could be explored, one operating in the long-term, the other two in the short-term.

The most urgent task nowadays is to work at building a Church where initiation is possible. It means we have to find what *type of community* can be valid for the Church today.

This concern has been the concern of many in recent years. It has not yielded many fruits because it has not been phrased in the correct perspective.

This community can no longer be the large society. This society is foreign to Christianity and we should not work at recapturing medieval christendom.

This community cannot be the family either, as the Christian family movements have seemed to advocate lately. First the family has become restricted to the nuclear family (Father, Mother, one or two children) and this limitation of vision and concern may have very little to do with Christianity indeed. In addition, the relationships of the child to his family are much too saturated with feelings and emotions for him to be able to get his autonomy with regard to religious beliefs and practices. If he knows Christ only through his parents the risk is great that when rejecting his parents in order to fully grow, he rejects Christianity at the same time.

This community cannot be the parish either, at least in urban areas. Our parishes are an inheritance of the past when our societies were mostly rural, when everyone during the week was sharing some kind of common life, where the people formed a human community before being a liturgical community. The present parishes have nothing in common with those former parishes save the name.

The future of Christian community therefore can only be a *free* gathering of people, composed of families, single parents, celibates, transcending neighbourhood or work-teams and brought together only in the name of shared Faith and Hope.

To be operative as initiating matrices they will have to meet the four following conditions:

A. They will have to be limited in number so that brotherhood/sisterhood among the members is visible to all including children. A membership of 50 — 80 seems to answer this condition according to the observations of social psychology.

B. Those communities cannot be limited to a spiritual dimension, because then they are no longer real human communities, displaying values in everyday life and capable of being matrices of initiation. Since community means sharing, there are three goods that these church communities should share besides prayer. One is *time*. If the people do not take time to be together, to talk together, to do things together, community will exist only on the verbal level. Another is *money*, *human goods*. Those communities must display a renunciation of the all-governing consumerist tendency by putting their possessions in common, at least partially: car, childcare, deep-freeze and so on. And finally they should share *culture*; in other words they should unite people who otherwise would be dispersed in separate boxes; they should make them open and tolerant; they should contribute to the freedom of the Kingdom of God here and now.

C. As we live in an instant-conscious era, those communities should not aim at being long-lasting, encompassing the whole life of people. They serve a limited purpose for a time and then are replaced by something else.

D. As they are small communities they cannot rely solely on the ordained priest for the maintenance of their existence and activities. Those communities will exist only if new ministries are conceived and accepted.

This description should not be a surprise to us because there are two models of them that have proved efficient. The first is the early communities of the Church of the first century which had all the characteristics described here. The second is the large Jewish family community which over several centuries down to our age has succeeded in transmitting the Faith without half of the special schools or of Sabbath classes.

We may even go one step further in our grasp of what should come. If we look at the history of the Church we find out that Religious life has sprung up only in the fourth and fifth century when a large segment of society had become Christian after Constantine. Prior to that it was the Christian communities that were the salt of the earth. The present difficulties of Religious communities are perhaps an invitation to think that we are faced with a pre-Constantine situation where it is the small communities of the Church as such that should embody at least partly the ideal of Religious life.

Another task that we have to undertake in between is to shift part of our resources, be they financial or people, from the field of the children and the young to the field of adult Religious Education. We do too much for the young and too little for the adults. This orientation is well underway, so it is unnecessary to dwell at length on it.

And finally when addressing ourselves to children we should adopt a form of speech fostering initiation.[5] Now the dilution of theological discourse which is still the basis of our catechetical content is not at all adapted to this objective. Theology gets its full meaning only when Faith pre-exists. Let us remember that people of God have been gathered and convocated by the kerygma and the narration of the great deeds of God to humanity. The children we get in our catechetical lessons have a unique character: they are baptised and as such should be able to get theological clarification of their Faith. But at the same

5. Cf. Claude and Jacqueline Lagarde — *Animer Une Équipe en Catéchèse*, Éd. le Centurion, this is one of the most creative studies of the use of Bible stories in Religious Education.

time they have a complete pagan mentality and value system and in this capacity they are unable to understand the things that are from God. Hence we have to introduce them first to the history of Salvation by adopting a much more narrative type of speech. This is what the Jewish families have been doing for ages with a success that is evident to everyone.

Let us point out that this narrative discourse does not need — as the theological one does — to be adapted to the various ages. It is a discourse that can be heard and understood by a whole people at a time. The wonder of narratives is that they can be re-intepreted over and over again along a lifetime, as they take new meaning through their confrontation with the growing experience of the listener.

Conclusion
It is to be hoped that following these orientations the Church would recover a balance that has been lost over the last twenty-five years, a balance between initiation and schooling that are both indispensable to a sound, whole education which addresses itself both to the cognitive and affective dimension of the person. At the same time it would heal the difference between theologians and pastors, a difference that has wounded the body of the Church since Vatican II.

Religious Education at the Crossroads

Michael J Wrenn

I am very happy and privileged to share some reflections with you here in Ireland, standing on the soil of my parents' birth. The title of my paper "Religious Education at the Crossroads" arises from the conviction that the almost twenty year long preoccupation with religious education by the Holy See and national hierarchies is indicative not merely of the central place which the catechesis of young people and adults plays in the life of the Church but also of the Church's underlying concern for the very future of its mission of evangelization and redemption.

This fundamental concern is observable in the number of documents on catechetics issued during the last twenty years which may be said to have culminated both in the Synod on Catechesis of 1977 and the publication in the United States of the National Catechetical Directory in the Spring of 1979.

Each of these events could be said to have been occasioned, in part, by the desire expressed in many quarters of the Church to analyze the direction which catechesis has been taking for almost a quarter of a century, and to provide the necessary framework and guidance for an orderly and unified approach to this task, so essential for the Church's future. In October of 1979, a definitive document *Catechesi Tradendae*, based on the results of the Synod of 1977, was published for the Church universal. This document, along with *Sharing the Light of Faith* (the National Catechetical Directory of the U.S.) should significantly contribute to a solution to the various meanderings which religious education has experienced during recent years. This paper, therefore, will explore two vital aspects of current catechesis — the progress that has been made on the theoretical level and the problem that remains on the practical level.

Any clear understanding of contemporary religious education must begin with a consideration of how the current official guidelines for catechesis came into being. The first part of this paper presents the context in which the National Catechetical Directory must be understood and examines the progress in religious education which this document represents. It is a matter of national record.

31

The NCCB Report in preparation for the Synod on Catechetics

In November of 1976, the National Conference of Catholic Bishops submitted a report to the General Secretariate of the Synod of Bishops for the Synod of 1977 which was scheduled to deal with the topic "Catechetics in our Time with Special Reference for Children and Young People". Data (obtained from a questionnaire designed by the NCCB Ad Hoc Committee for the Synod) which represented responses from forty nine dioceses in the U.S.A. formed the basis of the report submitted to the Holy See. Before investigating, in greater detail, the various theories and methodologies which have influenced the field of catechetics for more than two decades, it may be helpful to outline a number of the findings presented in the United States report. Our purpose would seem to be best served by considering what the report identifies as positive and negative developments in Catechesis during the last twenty or more years.

This time frame was singled out because the greatest number of changes in the field of religious education are alleged to have taken place during those years. The report indicated the general acceptance accorded the introduction into catechetics of developments occurring in the specialized areas of scripture, theology, patristics, liturgy, social doctrine and ecumenism. Next in importance and level of approval was the integration into catechesis of the findings of psychology, education, anthropology and sociology.

The use of experience, everyday situations, occurrences and problems, in short, experiential learning, was cited by many as a valuable means for assuring that the content of catechesis would be more readily understandable, practical and livable. The report observes: "The respondents saw this as the general acceptance of the inductive-experiential pedagogy as contrasted with deductive-abstract learning which has been emphasized over the last 500 years".[1]

Introduction into catechetics of developments in the ecclesiastical and human sciences, along with the employment of experiential learning, were said to have contributed significantly to the improvement of religious education methodologies, allowing them to develop from the informational, to the adaptive, to the kerygmatic and finally to the experiential emphasis approaches. It was also indicated that music, art, drama, mime, literature and apostolic activities have also been incorporated into the presentation of the message as a result of these contemporary methodologies. These vehicles of instruction were cited as producing a balance between the

---

1. National Conference of Catholic Bishops, "The State of Catechesis — Report to Synod Secretariate", April 27, 1977, Vol. 6, p 706.

communication of content and the tapping of emotional, intellectual, physical and motivational potentialities of the recipient of catechesis.

Textbooks were said to have benefitted from the introduction of the developments just mentioned. Movies, film-strips, records, tapes, cassettes, video-tapes, photos, posters, banners and art prints were said to "have enlarged the possibilities for effective communication".[2] The "professionalization" of catechists was considered next in order of importance and the report observed that the success of the catechetical programme on the local level is directly related to the presence of a "fulltime professionally trained catechist with leadership abilities".[3] The emergence of graduate schools of religious education, diocesan catechetical institutes and other training modalities for teacher preparation was approvingly commented upon by contributors to the report.

The growing involvement of parents in the catechesis of their children, especially in preparation for the reception of the first sacraments, was applauded and it was stated that programmes involving parents in the overall catechetical enterprise had proven to be most successful in the United States.

Approval of the recognition, in principle, of adult religious education as "an integral and indeed prime form" of catechesis was mentioned by many dioceses despite the mixed results in the success of these programmes. A fair number of respondents commented favourably upon a recent shift toward a more family-centred approach to catechetics and indicated that family religious education would be one of the major trends in the future.

The report discussed another significant trend, the growth of youth ministry which involves ministering to all the needs of the young person, including catechetical development. The effectiveness of "peer ministry", that is, ministry by temperamentally suited and properly trained persons who are about the same age as the youths being served, was discussed by a number of respondents.

Among other developments in catechetics which received some consideration in the report were the following: the realization that catechesis is a life-long process; the recognition that faith is a free choice rather than ethnic or cultural identification; the efforts to apply contemporary knowledge regarding the stages of human development to moral growth (Kohlberg); catechetical promotion of ecumenical awareness; concern for the evaluation of teaching content, methods and materials.

2. Loc. cit.
3. Loc. cit.

The report next considered developments during the last twenty years which have hindered catechesis. An initial observation was that many serious problems have actually been non-catechetical in origin or motive. Chief among these has been the breakdown in the cultural order. Since the United States may be said to have been distancing itself from at least a semblance of allegiance to and practice of Christian values, moving to the status of a secularized and, in many respects, amoral society, the Catholic community has been significantly influenced by such a trend.

In the view of the report, "this impact has been heightened by the breakup of many Catholic neighbourhoods and a movement to the suburbs".[4] Changes in society, such as the deterioration of the family, mounting divorce rates, one parent families, working mothers, the use of drugs, and abortion have also had a serious impact on the Catholic community.

The dramatic increase of recreational and educational opportunities competing with religious activities and especially religious education, was also termed important by several respondents.

The "confusion, ambiguity, distrust, fear and even hostility and anger produced by the changes that took place in the Church in the wake of the Second Vatican Council"[5] were considered the most serious handicaps to catechesis. The report went on to observe that while this was felt in all areas of Catholic life, religious education became one of the major battlegrounds for those who had opposing views on the Church and the world. Confusion led often to polarization and serious tensions between "progressives" and "conservatives". In several instances, the situation led to a crisis of faith and to disaffiliation from the Church.

Many dioceses reported that among the aspects of polarization affecting catechesis has been the division that developed between theologians and the magisterium.[6] This has resulted, in some cases, in the inability or failure of teachers to make a sufficiently clear distinction between matters of theological speculation and research and what is held and taught by the magisterium. It was noted that the process, in this regard, has filtered down from the level of university, seminary and college to elementary and secondary level religious education programmes.[7]

Interestingly enough, the report, in its concluding section, called

4. Ibid., p 707
5. Loc. cit.
6. Loc. cit.
7. Loc. cit.

for the establishment of dialogue between the hierarchy and scholars, particularly theologians. The report *unfortunately* conceded more responsibility to theologians than to bishops in this enterprise:

> Often the conclusions of theologians and the teachings of bishops do not agree. Since the theologian, and not the bishops, is the real teacher of the catechist, the former sets the tone for what is being taught in Catechesis at all levels, virtually throughout the country. This tension, if it is to be resolved, will require serious and extensive dialogue between theologians and bishops. There appears to be no other way of dealing with this real and serious problem.[8]

Blame for the ensuing confusion and polarization was assigned to the inadequate implementation of Vatican II and the ineffective communication of developments in the catechetical field. Changes were not accompanied by opportunities for all concerned to understand, internalize and participate in renewal. The report was quick to note, however, that this was equally true of parents and catechists as well as clergy and some religious.

Although some lauded modern catechetical textbooks, others criticized them, complaining that textbook series were "inaccurate, hurriedly written and foisted on the public" and lacked essential elements of doctrine and morality.[9] This contributed to the anti-intellectual approach of the late sixties and early seventies, a period sometimes referred to as the age of "glorious uncertainty". This produced, in the opinion of diocesan respondents to the report, nearly a whole generation "devoid of knowledge of the faith".[10] Such an approach implicitly denied that the committed Catholic is a thinking, rational being as well as "a feeling, desiring person".[11]

This existence of continued division regarding the cognitive versus the affective and the deductive versus inductive dimension of catechesis was also pointed out. Some maintained that cognitive and deductive approaches continue to dominate, so that religion is treated as a subject rather than a life to be lived, while others indicated that the affective and inductive approaches so dominate catechesis that psychological reactions rather than spiritual and intellectual growth are considered more important outcomes for the religious education enterprise. The abandonment of memorization as a legitimate pedagogical device was considered unfortunate by several respondents.

8. Ibid., p 723
9. Ibid., p 708
10. Loc. cit.
11. Loc. cit.

The tendency to substitute value clarification techniques for moral theology, to consider morality outside of a religious context and the Catholic tradition, and even to deny objective norms of morality, was strongly opposed by several respondents.

A number of dioceses observed that there had been a tendency to follow fads and to use gimmicks, gadgets, and novelties in catechesis. Frequent switching from one religious education programme to another with little or no continuity in scope and sequence has produced very negative results. Some lamented the tendency to view every new development in the field as a final answer instead of but one further element in catechesis requiring serious evaluation.[12]

The report indicated that the loss of credibility in the Church's mission, occasioned by the resignation of a significant number of priests and religious from their respective ministry and apostolate, proved harmful to catechesis. Complaints were also registered about the lack of pastoral support and supervision, a frequent result of priests abdicating their positions as those ultimately responsible for religious education programmes. The lack of professionally trained religious educators was also singled out as a negative element in the current field of religious education. Many have received neither theological nor pedagogical preparation to teach religion, a situation which impedes rather than encourages faith development. Selection of teachers is often made on the basis of availability without sufficient regard for their qualification.[13] A few reports noted that some catechists lack sensitivity and proper discretion in projecting their personal crisis such as those of vocation or faith and so disturbing the young people or adults whom they were teaching.

One hopeful element mentioned frequently in the report was the preparation of the *National Catechetical Directory*, about which we shall have more to say later.

The Way We Were — A Franco-American View

It will be helpful, at this point, to present an overview of the various influences on religious education in the United States during the last twenty years, especially an overview from the outside observer. Such an analysis should help us to get beneath the data which surfaced in the responses from diocesan officials and which were used to prepare the report just surveyed. In this task I am indebted to a too little publicized work entitled *The Resurgence of Religious Instruction*, 1977

---

12. Loc. cit.
13. Loc. cit.

by Brother Didier Jacques Piveteau, F.S.C., Professor of Catechetics at the Institute Catholique in Paris, who has been an astute observer of the American catechetical scene for nearly a quarter of a century, and Professor James T. Dillon, an educational psychologist from Chicago State University. *Resurgence* provides a suggestive framework for the analysis which follows.

Piveteau and Dillon entitle the first part of their work "Procession to Impasse, 1955-1975". The year 1955 is chosen since, in their view, this is the year when modern developments in catechetics began to happen in the United States. Up until this time, religious education was quite similar to what it had been before the second world war. But by 1955, religious educators in our country were beginning to be greatly influenced by European thought. Prominent catechists came to our shores from Germany, France and Belgium to give lectures and courses. In 1958 when Father Gerard Sloyan published the *Shaping the Christian Message*,[15] eight of the thirteen contributors were non-Americans.

Commenting upon the implications of the European influence, Piveteau and Dillon state that this receptivity to various European trends of thought "rested upon two assumptions which invite criticism. It presupposed first, that religious instruction was to be practised the same way throughout the world; second, that the theories of prominent thinkers either reflected or influenced practice at home or abroad".[16]Writing in the French edition of the International Catechetical review, *Lumen Vitae*, Piveteau, in an article, "Vingt Ans de Catechese Americaine", is even blunter: "Even in Europe the suggestion of these various pioneers were far from attracting the reception which Americans readily accorded to them. In fact, these authors were content enough merely not to be condemned."[17]
Commenting on the assumption that theory and practice necessarily go together, Piveteau and Dillon wrote:

> The writings of French thinkers imported by the United States, for example, were certainly a clouded picture of French practice

14. Didier, Jacques Piveteau, James T. Dillon, *Resurgence of Religious Instruction*, Religious Education Press, Notre Dame, Indiana, 1977.
15. Gerard S. Sloyan, ed., *Shaping the Christian Message : Essays in Religious Education*, MacMillan, New York, 1958.
16. Piveteau, Dillon, *Resurgence of Religious Instruction*, p 10.
17. Dider J. Piveteau, F.S.C., "Vingt Ans de Catéchèse Americaine" *Lumen Vitae* — (French Edition), 1977, Vol. 32. p 236. — "En réalité, même en Europe, les suggestions de ces pionniers étaient loin de trouver l'audience que les Américains leur prêtaient. Encore heureux quand ces auteurs n'etaient pas tout bonnement condamnés".

as a whole. Nor did they always succeed in having much to do with the state of affairs as these developed in their own country...[18]

In this connection, the authors suggest that Catholics were over eager to accept new pedagogical theories in order to attain "respectability".

The authors next consider the welter of confusing phases through which catechetics passed between 1960 and 1970: traditional, pedagogical, kerygmatic, existential, life-centred and group-centred (although this last phase is said to refer more to a European situation than one in our own country). The influences of International Catechetical Congresses between 1960 and 1968 are also surveyed and the conclusion reached that the Eichstatt (1960), Bangkok (1962) and Medellin (1968) Congresses represented kerygmatic, anthropological and political approaches respectively.[19]

A number of "turns for the worse" are treated especially with respect to the employment of methodological gimmickry during the 1960's. The sense of failure and despair experienced by many teachers of religion, during this period, is movingly described:

> The slow death of religion teachers transpired in several stages. The first two arose from experiencing external difficulties and consisted in turning upon one's students or one's tools; the last two arose from internal troubles and consisted in turning upon one's self, and then upon one's task...[20]

Finally, Dillon and Piveteau single out the writings of Alfonso M. Nebreda, S.J., and Gabriel Moran, F.S.C. as particularly noteworthy in this situation. In 1965, Alfonso Nebreda published his work, *Kerygma In Crisis?*[21] based principally upon his experience as a missionary in Japan where the proclamation of the Gospel message and the catechesis flowing from it no longer seemed to command attention. Nebreda proposed to resituate religious education by moving it out of its third phrase (catechesis) and concentrating on the very first phase, namely, pre-evangelization. Nebreda wrote: "I want to make it perfectly clear that the approach in pre-evangelization is radically different from the approach used in catechesis proper".[22] Whereas catechesis is christocentric, pre-evangelization is anthropocentric, allowing for facilitation of dialogue, respect for the individual and personal contact. Pre-evangelization corresponds to a

18. Piveteau, Dillon, *Resurgence of Religious Instruction*, p 11.
19. Ibid., p 26
20. Ibid., pp 32, 33
21. Alfonso M. Nebreda, *Kerygma in Crisis?*, Loyola, Chicago, 1965.
22. Ibid., pp 102, 103

model of counselling, while catechesis depends on instruction. Piveteau and Dillon remark on the difficulties involved with the translation of this theory into practice in the United States. The very term pre-evangelization is unfortunate since it arises out of a conception of theology "which separates the things of God and those of man. Explicit reference to Jesus Christ is withheld although individuals are implicitly experiencing the aegis and auspices of the Gospel".[23]

Nebreda furnished no procedures or strategies for translating his theories into practice. He seemed to be

> clearly naive and unsuspecting that to adopt a position as 'radical' as he himself describes it to be must entail an institutional upset in school and parish structure... In all likelihood, enough people were so frightened, resistant or overwhelmed by the institutional overhaul they detected between the lines that the message was prevented from ever being translated into practical terms.[24]

For Gabriel Moran, "the only thing which can save the catechetical movement from self-strangulation is to prepare teachers who have a theological understanding of Christian revelation".[25] In numerous publications, Moran has sought to set forth his view "at times obscurely and later on in a plainer and almost informal fashion".[26] Revelation can be viewed as "present in the life of every individual".[27] For Moran, revelation is a continuous, presently occurring process, not merely a collection of events from the remotest past. Although God did reveal in times past, God is revealing now, to me. God has spoken and God has saved — but also God is speaking and God is saving.[28]

Revelation is "neither doctrine nor message, but is a real, personal intercommunion"[29] and knowledge of revelation arises out of encounter and experience rather than from words and concepts. Yet, how is this concept to be translated into the educative process? As important as Moran considers this question, there is no effort to supply

23. Piveteau, Dillon, *Resurgence of Religious Instruction*, p 55.
24. Ibid., p 56
25. Gabriel Moran, *Catechesis of Revelation*, Herder and Herder, New York, 1966, p 151.
26. Piveteau, Dillon, *Resurgence of Religious Instruction*, p 58.
27. Gabriel Moran, F.S.C., *The Present Revelation : The Search for Religious Foundations*, Herder and Herder, New York, 1972, p 19.
28. Didier J. Piveteau, "Biblical Pedagogues". In James Michael Lee and Patrick C. Rooney (eds), *Toward a Future for Religious, Pflaum*, 1970, pp 83-114.
29. Gabriel Moran, *Catechesis of Revelation*, p 33.

an answer to it. His concern is with theology, not pedagogy and he claims that "the theology of revelation cannot solve the catechetical problem".[30] If Moran can be said to suggest a method, it would be to appeal to the student as a human person and to respect the person's free response. He also indicated the necessity to be less concerned with children and to concentrate on adults. Thus, he wrote: "I would question whether it is possible to overcome the obvious inadequacies of religion teaching so long as it is assumed that the teaching of Christianity is a child-centered endeavour. I see no evidence to suggest that Christianity can be taught well to little children and see no reason to suppose that one should try to teach it at all."[31]

After leading us over the paths taken by religious instruction from 1955 onward, which led to a number of blind alleys before coming to something of an impasse in the years 1965-1968, Dillon and Piveteau in a chapter entitled, "Enterprise at Rest", state:

> The picture is of an enterprise proceeding nowhere, now borrowing practices without shifting its fundamental mode of education, now proposing theological conceptions without re-working institutional structures accordingly, now taking approaches which violate underlying purposes and assumptions, now assuming views which contradict the approaches.[32]

In an effort to begin movement out of this unfortunate impasse in religious education, a number of dioceses in the U.S.A. saw fit to design religious education guidelines for school and non-school programmes. The guidelines were based upon such documents as the *General Catechetical Directory* (1971), the Bishops' Pastoral *To Teach as Jesus did*, and the NCCB's document *Basic Teachings for Catholic Religious Education* (1973). Questions addressed by the guidelines generally concerned the nature and goals of religious education programmes; the relationship of this enterprise to the Magisterium of the Church; the requisite qualities and competencies of catechists; teacher certification; roles and structures involved in programme implementation on the parish and diocesan level; and curriculum guidelines setting forth objectives for each grade of elementary and secondary school in areas of doctrine, scripture, liturgy, sacraments, prayer, moral development. This material was usually accompanied by corresponding learning activities and suggested opportunities for

---

30. Ibid., p 40
31. Gabriel Moran, Preface to Huber Halbias, *Theory of Catechetics: Language and Experiences in Religious Education*, Herder and Herder, 1971, pp 9, 10.
32. Piveteau, Dillon *Resurgence of Religious Instruction*, p 74.

Christian awareness and service appropriate to each grade level. In the words of one such diocesan venture:

> These guidelines are aimed at an adequate coverage of those elements of religious knowledge and the provision of those spiritual and liturgical experiences which will both contribute to and foster the students' development as informed Christians and provide them with the awareness of possessing a distinct Catholic identity in faith, worship, practice and discernment throughout their lives.[33]

It should be mentioned that these guidelines were elaborated more often than not as a result of the call by bishops, pastors, parents and teachers for assistance in their religious education efforts. Although several of these guidelines predated the consultation aimed at the preparation of the National Catechetical Directory, they nevertheless looked forward to the further precisions to be derived from the ultimate publication of what is now known as *Sharing the Light of Faith*. It is to this monumental national religious education undertaking that we must now turn our attention.

Project Rainbow — the N.C.D.
The bishops of the United States, at their April 1972 meeting, voted to commission the development of a National Catechetical Directory. This was to fulfill the prescriptions of the *General Catechetical Directory* and to apply it's principles to the circumstances of the U.S.A.

The document was to be prepared by means of widespread consultation with the Church at large, as well as with scholars and the bishops themselves. There were three phases to the consultation. The first (December 1973 — March 1974) was intended to be an educational process for the purpose of securing suggestions from parents, priests, religious and religion teachers regarding which areas should be covered by the Directory. Publishers and national organizations involved in religious education also contributed to this phase. Over seventeen thousand suggestions from the consultation contributed to the composition of the first draft, 650,000 copies of which was circulated between January — April, 1975. The second phase yielded 765,300 recommendations for improving the document and this data, after being computerized and analyzed, became the basis for the revision of the first draft. This revision was distributed in the

---

33. Office of the Director of Religious Education, Department of Education, Archdiocese of New York, "The Faith that marks God's People", 1976, p 1.

Spring of 1977 for a similar consultative go-around. Recommendations for the third consultation became the basis for the preparation by the directory committee of the final draft which would be submitted to the bishops at their Fall (November 14 — 17, 1977) meeting. Some 350 amendments to the final drafts were submitted by the bishops and were voted upon in the course of the meeting. The amendment process proved, in several respects, to be essential. Up until that time, there was a growing feeling that with each succeeding draft's attempt to be acceptable to the various and even opposing positions held by religious educators on a number of important issues and topics, the overall effectiveness and credibility of the final version was being seriously compromised. One has hailed the genius of the draft text, "which can, within one and the same paragraph encompass not only both extremes but numbers of middles, delivering itself of the whole with such ineffable finesse that all parties can think themselves unambiguously either sustained or stranded in their views".[34]

More than 100 amendments were approved by way of adding, deleting or amending paragraphs and sections of the Directory. Although some of these revisions were principally stylistic, a number of them altered the Directory significantly and for the better in several key sections. On November 17, 1977 the bishops, by a vote of 216 in favour to 12 opposed, directed that the document be sent to Rome for approval. A few, reacting to the amendment process, expressed the view that the bishops had "almost ravaged the Directory" or had "turned it around 140 degrees". Such reactions were probably from unofficial sources, although quoted in the *National Catholic Reporter*.

In a letter dated October 30, 1978, and addressed to Archbishop John Quinn, President of the National Conference of Catholic Bishops, the Sacred Congregration for the Clergy commended *Sharing the Light of Faith* for:

> being a generally faithful application of the General Catechetical Directory to the American ecclesial spirit, its clarity of expression, its emphasis on memorization of basic prayers and doctrinal formulations, its solid argument, its flexibility. The substantial orthodoxy of *Sharing the Light of Faith* should be apparent to anyone who studies the entire work attentively. Doctrinal statements that may seem incomplete at first reading of one section are habitually rounded out in another.[35]

34. Piveteau, Dillon, *Resurgence of Religious Instruction*, p 214.
35. Sacred Congregation for the Clergy, Second Office, Prot. No. 158897/11, "Letter of October 30, 1978 to Archbishop John Quinn, President of the National Conference of Catholic Bishops". *Origins*, Vol. 8, p 374.

Having delivered itself of these initial encomiums, the letter went on to indicate that "there are certain points of importance that should be reworked before the publication of the first edition".[36]

Regarding the compromise position which the authors of the Directory had taken on the question of revelation employing a capital "R" to refer to that public revelation which closed at the end of the apostolic age as opposed to the use of a lower case "r" for the revelation other than public revelation, the letter observed:

> the employment of capital and small letters (Revelation, revelation) to distinguish various meanings of the notion of revelation tends to engender confusion. It would seem to be less open to misunderstanding, if the word 'revelation' standing alone, without modifiers, quotation marks or italics, were to signify public, divine revelation in the strict sense, and that other expressions be chosen to indicate other modes by which God manifests himself to men.[37]

Likewise, on the position adopted by the directory committee regarding the question of preparation for the reception of the Sacrament of Penance and First Eucharist, the letter observed: "Not only should the Catechesis for the Sacrament of Reconciliation precede First Holy Communion, but youngsters should normally receive the Sacrament of Penance before their First Communion".[38]

The section of the Directory which dealt with the administration of General Absolution was said to require the reflection of existing norms by indicating more clearly that General Absolution is not only to be rarely extended but also that the circumstances determining its administration should be serious. The specific nature of the priesthood was shown to need a more exact expression by placing appropriate emphasis on both its sacrificial Eucharistic aspect, and on the concept of the configuration of the priest to Christ. The ministerial priest acts not only in the name of Christ but "in the person of Christ". Also, the character of the priest and bishop was cited as needing to be more clearly distinguished from that of the deacon as well as from the common priesthood of the faithful, which differs from the ministerial or hierarchical priesthood "essentially and not only in degree".[39]

Probably one of the most crucial areas of concern is that bearing upon the very nature of the religious education enterprise itself. In the final draft of the N.C.D., the term religious education was dropped

36. Loc. cit.
37. Loc. cit.
38. Ibid., p 374
39. Loc. cit.

in favour of the term catechesis. The fact that both of these expressions were not to be chosen for use, even interchangeably in the text, was a significant victory for those, during the last twenty years, who claimed that religious education programmes are stifled when measured against the yardstick of school structures. Much of this persisting debate can be summed up in the broader question of whether catechesis is a pastoral or an educational function. Actually, both functions would seem to be involved — the pastoral function being philosophically and organizationally presupposed by the educational; the educational being instrumentally necessary to the pastoral. To deny that catechesis is an educational function is to deny that it is to achieve cognitive, attitudinal and behavioural changes leading to growth and development in the Christian life. The object of pastoral care, which can also be described as a process of religious socialization, is Christian "nurturing", to use a term borrowed from a number of Protestant religious educators and widely used in Catholic religious education circles today.

One means necessary, one which religious education represents, is a systematic effort to achieve cognitive, attitudinal and behavioural responses in the student which contribute to his formation. The pastoral dimension is both contextual and casual. It is also concerned simultaneously with the process of both structuring and nurturing — to use the terminology of James Michael Lee and John Westerhoff respectively. Pastoral aim, motive, and ultimately evaluation are the context, the formal and final causes, as it were, of catechesis. Catechesis, then is the systematic, instrumental carrying out of pastoral intent which is Christian formation.

Good News and Bad News — Efforts at Evaluation
In the Spring of 1976, a special task force of the National Catholic Educational Association was convened to prepare a Religious Education Outcomes Inventory (REOI) consisting of a ninety item religious knowledge inventory and a forty item religious/moral catalogue. The religious knowledge inventory was designed to yield individual and class profiles in five areas, (1) God, Father, Son, Spirit; (2) Church: Community of Believers; (3) Sacraments: Initiation, Community Reconciliation; (4) Christian Life: Witness and Service; (5) Scripture: Living Word of God. The attitude measure was to report, item by item, group responses on attitudes relating to the same five areas. Drawing upon the *General Catechetical Directory*, the current draft of the N.C.D., *Basic Teachings, To Teach as Jesus Did*, the N.C.E.A. Curriculum Guide for Continuous Progress in Religious Education Programmes, and major textbooks presently being used.

The special N.C.E.A. Task Force selected the contents and items for the REOI. This instrument was designed for use by school and G.C.D. programmes in the junior high, but ideally in the eighth grade level. Generally accepted by school administrators and personnel, the utilization of the inventory was initially and continues to be challenged by a number of professionals responsible for non-school religious education programmes locally and nationally. The REOI has been administered to over 50,000 students from nearly 100 dioceses and 3,000 institutions across the country.

Writing in the June 1978 Newsletter of the NCEA of Religious Educators, Father Alfred McBride, O.Praem, NCEA Religious Education Forum Directory, presented a report on the REOI results of 1978. In that report he expresses concern about the religious illiteracy of many, a lack of awareness and understanding concerning the codewords of Christianity, and the existence of imprecision in the basics of liturgy and scripture.[40]

The appearance of such an evaluative instrument as the Religious Education Outcomes Inventory augured well for continued attempts to assure that the catechetical enterprise will be concerned with promoting those cognitive and attitudinal outcomes which will contribute to a young person's growth and development in the Catholic faith tradition.

But there is one further area which is probably more essential than any other. It is that of the organization, supervision and management of the religious education task. As one surveys the last two decades of religious education in North America it becomes increasingly apparent that a crucial element in the overall enterprise seems to have bogged down. Institutional expectations, comprising not merely those key expectations of the Bishop and his diocesan office, but also the expectations reflected by parents, priests and parishioners, as well as administrators and teachers, often seemed to differ significantly from the institutional expectations of religious education theoreticians in graduate and undergraduate programmes, textbook authors and publishers and even some individual teachers in school and CCD programmes. In organizational terms, there no longer appeared to be an adequate interactional flow between institutional expectations on the normative level and the personal or ideographic expectations of those serving the religious education enterprise in various capacities.

40. Alfred McBride, O.Praem., "Less than 60%... Or Everything You Didn't Want to Know About Their Answers", *NCEA, Religious Education Newsletter Forum*, June, 1978. Vol. 5, pp 1-3.

Such an interactional flow is essential to the proper achievement of goals and outcomes within the social system.[41]

To a great extent, *Sharing the Light of Faith*, through its process of consultation, initiated this interactional flow for the first time on the national level. However, theoreticians in the field, individual catechists, religious teaching communities, textbook publishers, graduate schools of religious education, will constantly need to evaluate themselves as to whether or not their contribution to the field actually responds to those expectations which parents, parish communities, and bishops have the responsibility of determining for the religious education of young people and adults.

These expectations, by necessity, have to be in accordance with the faith and practice of the Church as well as generally accepted pedagogical theory reflected in acceptable tried and proven methodologies. Attention to the formulation of various strategies to foster a partnership between those in authority and those in the field could contribute greatly to the attainment of a unified approach to religious education in the United States. The lack of such a partnership constitutes the great problem in religious education today, a problem which must be carefully examined in order to be addressed.

Unfortunately the lack of such a partnership still constitutes a great problem in religious education circles in the U.S., *The National Catechetical Directory* or *Catechesi Tradendae* notwithstanding.

What follows will be a number of possible reasons for this situation.[42] But before doing so, now would seem to be the moment for total candour.

Let's face it, let's own up to it. It is about time that we become deadly serious and admit what is being admitted in a number of secular fields of education, namely that there is an absolute necessity to return to the basics in these fields and if this is the case in these fields, all the more reason for doing so in this most important field of religious education.

In what will undoubtedly be hailed as a classic description of the contemporary Roman Catholic Church, Joseph Cardinal Ratzinger observes in his *Report on the Faith*:

> Just as theology no longer seems even to transmit a common model of the faith, so catechesis is being exposed to piece-mealing, cutting up, and to experiences which continually

41. J. W. Getzels and E. G. Guba, "Social Behaviour and the Administrative Process", *School Review*, Vol. 65, 1957, pp 423-41.
42. Monsignor Michael J. Wrenn "Synod's Particular Questions", in *Fellowship of Catholic Scholar Newsletter*, September 1985, Vol. 8, pp 12, 13.

change. Certain catechisms and numerous catechists no longer teach the Catholic faith in its harmonious whole (a constant refrain of John Paul II in *Catechesi Tradendae* — in which each truth presupposes and explains the following — but they seek to make humanly 'interesting' (according to the fancy of cultural orientations of the moment) certain elements of the Christian patrimony. Particular biblical passages are focused upon because they are considered as 'closer to contemporary sensibility'. Others, for the opposite reason, are laid aside. In other words, there is no longer a catechesis which would be an overall, global formation in the faith, but reflections or inspirations drawn from partial and subjective anthropological experiences.[43]

In January of 1983 Ratzinger delivered a conference (which caused a great stir in Paris and Lyon) on the "new catechesis". It was entitled *Transmission of the Faith and Source of the Faith*. On this occasion, with his customary clarity, he declared among other things:

It was a fundamental and serious mistake to suppress the catechism, calling it passé. He spoke in this regard of an erroneous decision, promoted on an international scale precipitously and with great assurance.[44]

In his book Cardinal Ratzinger continues:

It is important to recall that from the earliest periods of Christianity there appeared a permanent and irreducible 'nucleus' of catechesis and therefore of formation in the faith. It is the same nucleus employed by Luther for his catechism, which is also that of the Roman catechism decided upon at Trent. The entire exposition on Faith is organized around four basic element: The *Credo*, the *Our Father*, the *Ten Commandments* and the *Sacraments*. This is the basis of the life of the Christian; this is the synthesis of the teaching of the Church based on Scripture and Tradition. The Christian finds there what he is *to believe* (the Symbol or Credo), *to hope for* (the Our Father), *to do* (The Ten Commandments) and the vital space in which all of this is to be accomplished *(the Sacraments)*. But, in so many cases of present day catechesis, this basic structure is abandoned, with the results that we all know: a disintegration of the *sensus fidei* among the

43. Joseph Cardinal Ratzinger, Vittorio Messori, *Entretien Sur La Foi*, Librairie Arthime Fayare, Paris, 1985, pp 83, 84.
44. Joseph Cardinal Ratzinger, *Transmission of the Faith and Sources of the Faith*, translated by Monignor Michael J. Wrenn, for *The Wanderer*, April 1985, *Wanderer Supplement*, p 3; Ratzinger and Messorio *p. cit*, pp 83, 84.

young generations, often incapable of an overall vision of their religion.[45]

Ratzinger goes on further to put his finger on what many see as bedevilling the catechetical enterprise, namely, the notion that it is possible to take a position "in favour" of Vatican II and "against" the Council of Trent and Vatican I. He shows clearly that the Second Vatican Council belongs to no one group as such. It belongs to God and his Church. Whoever accepts Vatican II, such as it is, clearly expressed and understood, affirms at the same time the entire uninterrupted tradition of the Catholic Chuch, and in particular the preceding two Councils.[46]

Speaking on August 25th at Rimini at the annual meeting of the Italian organization *Communione e Liberazione*, my own Cardinal, Archbishop of New York, John J. O'Connor, spoke of the need to distinguish between correct and incorrect pluralism. He described orthodoxy as:

> dynamic, as truth is dynamic. It needs no defences, any more than truth needs defences. It needs no apology, any more than does truth. It must be taught as truth itself, shouted from the housetops. It is not to be whispered behind barriers, fearful of attack, or cowed by ridicule... God's people have an absolute right, in justice, to the truth of such teachings and a critical need to hear it taught gently but charitably, but firmly, clearly and courageously.[47]

In a penetrating analysis of Cardinal Ratzinger's address at Paris and Lyon published in *Angelicum* in 1985, Msgr. Eugene Kevane, former Dean of the School of Education of the Catholic University of America and one of the pioneers in the development of Pontifical Catechetical Institutes in North America, gives as one possible reason for the suppression of the Catechism the following explanation:

> The transcendent God of Revelation begins to suffer philosophical eclipse. Philosophy is separated from religion and becomes a secular subject. Furthermore, by universal methodical doubt, I separate myself from the tradition of my ancestors and build up by myself with my new tool all the knowledge and wisdom I need for human life in the cosmos... There is no intelligent and transcendent Supreme Being, distinct from the cosmos, who can declare his thoughts to man, as the Prophet

45. Ratzinger and Messori, op. cit, pp 83, 84.
46. Ibid., p 29
47. John Cardinal O'Connor "Dynamic Orthodoxy", *Catholic New York*, August 29, 1985, p 23.

Amos says. The phrophetic light is snuffed out because the divine light is asserted not to exist. What then of the Bible? Where it seems to bear witness to intervention from beyond this cosmos, it must be explained by a new atheistic hermeneutic. Religious faith is replaced by philosophical facts: I believe in my self, in my own thinking, in my own demonstration of rational ethics. Catechesis, the receiving of a word on the authority of God revealing, is replaced by a different kind of religious education understood as an on-going 'faith-experience' of life within the cosmos.[48]

At about the same time as the French translation of Cardinal Ratzinger's "Report" appeared, the second edition of *Pierres Vivantes* a "Collection of privileged documents of the Faith" for use in French catechetical programmes was published. The first edition was modified as a result of the intervention of the Sacred Congregations for the Doctrine of the Faith and the Clergy. Nevertheless Cardinal Ratzinger's congregation saw fit to list a number of further necessary changes regarding Inspiration, Original Sin, Justice, Grace, Eucharist, The Cross, Sacrifice, Church, *Memorial*, (it is necessary to speak of the real presence of Jesus in the sacrament), Redemption, Liberation, the Role of the Pope. In most instances the treatment of these topics was considered vague, ambiguous and misleading.

In his letter to the French hierarchy, Ratzinger notes that since *Pierres Vivantes* is not being presented as a catechism, the suggestions made for the improvement do not constitute the preliminary approval on the part of the Holy See set forth in Comm. 775 of the Revised Code. The Cardinal then suggests that maybe what is most needed in France is "a catechism for the entire nation which, in a complete manner, presents the doctrine of the faith".[49]

Continuing his own analysis of the reason for the crisis in Catechesis in various parts of the world, your late revered shepherd, Archbishop Dermot Ryan, raised a series of very penetrating questions in Paris and Lyon in 1983.

> Why not ask if the heart of the doctrine had been correctly taught? Has it been presented with a clarity, an insistence, an adequate explanation? Has a good effort been made to have students learn this basic minimun which they will be able to use

48. Monsignor Eugene Kevane, "Toward Research in Fundamental Catechetics", *Angelicum* Vol. 62, 1985, p 374.
49. Joseph Cardinal Ratzinger, "Lettre du Cardinal Ratzinger au President de la Conference Episcopale Francaise", in *L'Homme Nouveau*, Juillet-Aout, 1985, p 8.

later on when they have to face the demands of their Christian lives as adults? Youth needs to be provided with the principle reference points of the landscape of their faith.[50]

Yes, Religious Education, Catholic Education finds itself at the Crossroads. What follows are a number of suggestions which might be acted upon in the future.

1. Bishops in the United States need to take direct responsibility for the enterprise of Religious Education in their dioceses. Diocesan directors have, in many instances, coopted the teaching function of Bishops. They should be known as diocesan advisers, rather than directors.

2. There should be one textbook series, K-12, published under the direct auspices of the Bishops of the United States. Guidance from a Holy See Reference Text for religious education programmes would be helpful.

3. There should be a Holy See conducted evaluation of Graduate and Undergraduate Schools of Religious Education in North America and elsewhere. This should be called for at the Synod in 1985.

4. The Extraordinary Synod should once and for all clarify the Church's position on dissent and charitably invite reverential and obedient submission.

5. There needs to be a series of clarifications regarding Scriptural Inspiration, Inerrancy, the Nature of Revelation. Historicity in the New Testament and the manner of reconciling Faith and Exegesis.

6. An International Catechetical Congress should be convened by the Holy See (Sacred Congregation for Catholic Education and Sacred Congregation for Clergy) no later than Spring 1988 for the purpose of setting forth uniform guidelines regarding goals and objectives in the field of Catechetics and Religious Education. The question of professionalism needs to be thoroughly studied and needed correctives presented in order to re-establish a relationship between the religious educator, the local pastor, the Bishop and the Holy Father.

7. The Extraordinary Synod should set a timetable for proper education about the Church's position on matters of faith and morals which have been misrepresented over the last twenty years. The Church Universal must re-establish a proper interactional flow

---

50. Mgr. Dermot J. Ryan, "Dégager les leçons du passé" in *Transmettre la foi aujourd' hui*, Centurion, Paris, 1983, p 23

between its stated institutional educational goals and the perception of these goals by those serving their implementation: bishops, priests, theologians, religious educators, etc.[51]

Allow me to conclude my presentation by sharing with you a very personal and deeply moving remembrance of Archbishop Fulton J. Sheen. In 1976, I had invited him to tape an Instructional Television programme on the *Meaning of the Eucharist in My Life* in preparation for the Eucharistic Congress in Philadelphia that year. It was aimed at junior high and high school students (11-18 year olds). His presentation was done to perfection and when the lights went up in the studio at the conclusion, I began to hear weeping and looked about only to find a young student technician with her head buried in her hands. I approached her to ask if I could be of assistance and as her tear filled eyes met mine she said: "But, Father, he really believes". Scripture scholars are beginning to tell us that when we translate the Greek New Testament verb "pisteuein" by our English word "believe", a real disservice is done because the modern English word "believe" designates a weak, waffling who pays his money, takes his choice, and gives assent. It does not designate the certitude about the truth implied in the Hebrew root of the word in its derivative *Amen* which means absolute certainty regarding the truth.

"But, Father, he really believes". Could any greater tribute be paid to you or to me for our past, present and future efforts in handing on the one true Faith which we received originally from those eyewitnesses and ministers of the Word, but in a special way from those saints and scholars and humble yet profound peasant folk of this blessed land who exulted in it, suffered and died for it and still managed to carry it proudly and without apology to four corners of the earth? I think not.

51. Monsignor Michael J. Wrenn, op.cit., *"Fellowship of Catholic Scholars Newsletter"* September, 1985. p 13.

PART TWO

Special Questions Facing Religious Education

Catechetical Directory or Catechism?
Une Question Mal Posée.

Berard L. Marthaler, OFMConv.

On the eve of the Extraordinary Synod of Bishops convened by Pope John Paul II to mark the twentieth anniversary of the adjournment of the second Vatican Council many were apprehensive that the meeting would cool the enthusiasm and perhaps even reverse the direction of *aggiornamento* inspired by Pope John XXIII's keynote address. Pope John had found in the signs of the times indications that Divine Providence was leading the Church to new opportunities for spreading the gospel message. Although he did not approve of everything that was happening, "We feel," he said, "we must disagree with those prophets of gloom, who are always forecasting disaster, as though the end of the world were at hand."[1] In 1985, however, voices of gloom were being heard on all sides, some expressing fear that the bark of Peter was once again in danger of capsizing, some anticipating that the Synod would betray the ideals and advances of the Council. Bishop after bishop felt it necessary to reassure all who would hear that the Synod would not, indeed did not have the authority to, repudiate the reforms initiated by Vatican II.

And now, in the wake of the Synod, many continue to be apprehensive. They are heartened by the fact that the Synod explicitly endorsed "the great importance and timelessness of the Pastoral Constitution *Gaudium et Spes*," and reaffirmed the basic ideals and strategies for renewal. Even the critics of the Synod admit that the statement issued at the close of the Synod commits the Church to the principles of Vatican II for years to come. It is when they look beyond the generalities, however, to the suggestions for specific action which conclude each section of the documents that they become apprehensive. They point in particular to one recommendation, namely, "the desire that a catechism or compendium of all Catholic doctrine regarding both faith and morals be composed" (II, B 4). In itself this suggestion seems innocuous, even wholesome, if it were not

---

1. Walter M. Abbott, *The Documents of Vatican II*. New York: America Press, 1966; p. 712.

55

for the fact that the compilation of such a compendium seems to run counter to the spirit if not the letter of the Second Vatican Council. The idea of a universal catechism had come up in the preparatory phase, even before the Council convened, but commissions, after considering various aspects of the issue, mandated instead the issuance of a General Catechetical Directory. [2]

The first Vatican Council had spent more time debating the desirability and feasibility of a universal catechism than it did discussing papal infallibility. In the end Vatican I approved but never formally promulgated the decree *De Parvo Catechismo* which called for a universal catechism for children along the lines of the Bellarmine catechism in use in Rome. During the preparatory phase of Vatican II Bishop Lacointe of Beauvais, anticipating that many of his brother bishops would return to the unfinished project *De Parvo Catechismo*, urged instead the compilation of a catechetical directory which would establish principles and general norms to serve as guidelines for catechesis. He argued that a single catechism for the universal Church was not possible or, at least, not proper. Ultimately the Preparatory Commission *de disciplina cleri et populi Christiani* endorsed the idea of a directory which would describe the goals of catechesis, the principle tenets of doctrine and, the wording of formulas. It would leave to episcopal conferences the implementation of the general norms and their application to specific situations.

The Preparatory Commission adopted the position that a single catechism for the universal Church was not feasible *(non exedire)*. The proposed directory would instead lay down "rules and general norms, which would have to be observed in compiling individual catechisms." *The General Catechetical Directory (GCD)*, moreover, when finally published, did not abolish catechisms but rather stated "the greatest importance must be attached to catechisms." The *GCD* not only stated the norms which must govern the contents of catechisms, but it also made some practical suggestions to guide their compilation (par. 119; see also par 134). Later, in his apostolic exhortation *Catechesi Tradendae*, Pope John Paul II encouraged episcopal conferences "to prepare genuine catechisms which will be faithful to the essential

2. I recount the development of the directory in *Catechetics in Context. Notes and Commentary on the General Catechetical Directory*. Huntington, IN.: Our Sunday Visitor, 1973; pp. xvi-xxx. See also Michael Donnellan, "Bishops and Uniformity in Religious Education: Vatican I to Vatican II," *Living Light* 10(1973): 237-238; reprinted in Michael Warren, ed., *Sourcebook for Modern Catechetics*. Winona, MN: St. Mary's Press, 1983; pp 232-243.

content of revelation and up to date in method, and which will be capable of educating the Christian generations of the future to a sturdy faith." Others who assume the serious responsibility of preparing catechetical materials, "especially catechism texts," he said, "can do so only with the approval of the pastors who have the authority to give it." They must conform as closely as possible to norms set down in the *General Catechetical Directory* "which remains the standard reference" (par. 50).

Thus to play off the catechetical directory against the catechism as if it were a choice of one or the other leads inevitably to polarization. It is simply *une question mal posée* that distorts the issues. Many (myself included), who have been lukewarm to the idea of a new generation of catechisms, are opposed not to catechisms in themselves but to the idea that new catechisms, however inspirational and informative, are perceived as a panacea for all that ails the catechetical ministry. A history of catechesis from the sixteenth century to the present that follows the trail of catechisms finds that there are families of catechisms. Such a history shows, moreover, that the need to adapt catechisms to specific circumstances, different cultures and age groups, led to the proliferation of catechisms. Despite the fact that almost all Catholic catechisms up to recent years showed some familiar traits of the Tridentine catechism and most were lineal descendents of the works of Peter Canisius and Robert Bellarmine (though as Father Wallace whom we honour in these lectures has shown, the catechism of James Butler II, archbishop of Cashel, sired a number of descendents in the English-speaking world), critics emphasized the differences rather than the similarities. It might be well to review briefly the history of catechisms before we commit all our resources to implementing the Synod's recommendation. Such a survey, moreover, will illustrate why I would be uneasy about being forced to choose between a catechetical directory and a catechism. It will also be helpful in pointing out an important difference between the decree *De Parvo Catechismo* of Vatican I and the recommendation of the 1985 Synod of Bishops.

The Catechism in History[3]
Catechisms in the modern sense are of fairly recent vintage. They first appeared with the Reformation. Martin Luther published two catechisms, a "Large Catechism" for the use of pastors and teachers

3.   See, E. Germain, *2000 ans d'éducation de la foi*. Belgium: Desclee, 1983; pp 81-93, 103-109, J-C Dhotel, *Les origines du catéchisme moderne*. Theologie 71. Paris: Aubier, 1967. F. Cors, "Catechisms," in *New Schall-Herzog Encyclopedia of Christian Knowledge*, II, pp.442-449.

and a "Small Catechism" for the common people and children. Luther's works were concise, clear expositions of the Ten Commandments, the articles of the Creed, the Lord's Prayer and Baptism, Holy Communion and Confession. The Small Catechism was cast in the form of questions and answers readily adapted to rote memorization.

The official character of Luther's catechisms is recognized in the *Book of Concord* of 1580. There they are published with the traditional creeds — Apostle, Nicene and Athanasian — along with the Augsburg Confession and other foundational documents of the Lutheran community. In the Protestant tradition the popular catechism enjoys something of an official status as a confessional document, a doctrinal statement that delineates basic tenets. As one studies the large catechisms of the Reformation and Counter-Reform, it is evident that they were intended to be reference works for use by clergy — preachers and teachers — rather than manuals of instruction to be put into the hands of ordinary faithful and catechists. The Heidelberg Catechism, for example, still in regular use in several churches in Europe and North America, was accepted by sixteenth-century Calvinists as an authoritative exposition of Reformed doctrine. Purposefully designed to allow many interpretations, it gradually supplanted Calvin's Geneva Catechism. In the seventeenth century, the Longer and Shorter Catechisms of the Westminster Assembly (1647) explicated the Westminster Confession of Faith and thus came to be regarded as a confessional statement and a test of orthodoxy among Presbyterians.

The Catechism of the Council of Trent corresponds in form and purpose to Luther's Large Catechism. The Council Fathers, says the preface, "were not satisfied with having decided the more important points of Catholic doctrine against the heresies of our time, but deemed it further necessary to deliver some fixed form of instructing the faithful in the truths of religion — a form to be followed by those to whom are lawfully entrusted the duties of pastor and teacher."[4] Despite a few remarks of this kind in the preface, the Tridentine Catechism is not openly polemical. The text makes it obvious, however, that the authors were sensitive to the issues that the Protestants had brought into dispute. The authors recognized that the manner of communicating the faith is of considerable importance, and that

4. *The Catechism of the Council of Trent.* Translated by J. Donovan. New York: Christian Assoc. Publishing Co., 1905; p. 15. Donovan, a professor at Royal College, Maynooth, dated his introduction, June 10, 1829. See, P. Rodriguez and R. Lanzetti, *El Catecismo Romano: Fuentes e historia del texto y de la redaccion.* Pamplona: Eds Universidad de Navarra, 1982.

instruction needed to be adapted according to the "age, capacity, manners and condition" of the learners. Thus they left it to local ordinaries and private enterprise to adapt the *Catechismus ad Parrochos* for the faithful and children.

Even before the Council of Trent commissioned a catechism, however, the zealous and learned St. Peter Canisius (1521-1597) recognized the need for a concise statement of Catholic teaching. Following the lead of Luther, Canisius produced Large and Small Catechisms, as well as one of medium length. The theological controversies of the Reformation provided the backdrop for the catechism of Peter Canisius, but he undertook to refute Protestant errors in the way he structured his works and by the issues he raised rather than engage in open polemics.

Though the Tridentine Catechism did not appear until 1566, it had been mandated twenty years earlier in one of the Council's first actions. It is significant that it was conceived at the same time the Council began drafting a decree on preaching and, in fact, the Tridentine catechism was intended to be a reference manual for preachers. It was to be "drawn from Scripture and the Orthodox Fathers, containing only matters of faith." In its own way it represented as much of a departure from the Augustinian sequence as did Luther's catechism. The Tridentine catechism, whose principal authors were three Dominicans, reflects a Thomistic understanding of the relationship between the elements of Christian doctrine: (1)faith and the Creed; (2)the sacraments; (3)the decalogue; and (4) the Lord's Prayer. By linking the sacraments with the Creed, the Roman catechism subtly but clearly sets Catholic teaching regarding faith and sacraments apart from that of many of the Reformers.

Bellarmine's Catechism

The Catechism of the Council of Trent, addressed as it was to the clergy, was not the answer to the popular catechisms of the Protestants. Edmund Auger's refutation (1563) of the catechism of John Calvin served its purpose in French-speaking countries, and Canisius's work continued to be popular in German-speaking lands. Their circulation, however, seems to have been limited to north of the Alps. In the Mediterranean countries, especially Italy, the catechetical works of Robert Bellarmine (1542-1621) held sway.

Bellarmine's two catechisms, the *Dottrina cristiana breve*, (1597) and the *Dichiarazione più copiosa della dottrina cristiana* (1598), grew out of the instructions he gave to the brother coadjutors of the Society of Jesus. His theological framework and general orientation differ markedly from that of Canisius. Bellarmine's definitions are more concise; the number of references to Scripture are fewer. The catechisms are coherent with Bellarmine's theological system. The kind of institutional ecclesiology associated with his name is evident; they are oriented toward the visible, hierarchical church. The authority of Rome is held up as a sure guide. Undoubtedly Bellarmine's catechisms owed their success in large part to the endorsement of Pope Clement VIII, but much of their popularity is due to the fact that they were more consonant with the theology — especially the ecclesiology — of the post-Tridentine period than the works of Canisius and the later catechism of Claude Fleury.

The Tridentine Catechism is remarkably free from polemics but it was still shaped by the controversies of the time. In many ways richer than the Council statements themselves, the issues it addresses were in large part the bones of contention between Catholics and Protestants. There was also a negative side in using the catechism for apologetic purposes. "To have learnt the catechism against someone," argues Henri deLubac in *Catholicism*, lead to a "narrowness of outlook and lack of proportion" that is tantamount to error. He points out, for example, that for a long time after Luther, catechisms were silent about "Christian liberty" and spoke of the Mass as if it were a sacrifice in some sort of way independent of Calvary.[5]

But long before Lubac pointed up the inadequacy of catechisms as confessional documents, Claude Fleury (1640-1725), the renowned church historian, criticized catechisms as instructional tools. In the lengthy Introduction to his *Catéchisme historique* Fleury indicts the way they presented "the first elements of Christianity."[6] Fleury is concerned to justify his own method, that is, a narrative of salvation, which he says takes its inspiration from St. Augustine's *De Catechizandis Rudibus*. His main criticisms of the catechisms were two that would recur again and again: (1) They were compositions of theologians and scholars whose logic and language (even when rendered in the vernacular) were beyond children and the unlettered; and (2) catechisms had come to be regarded as books to be read and even memorized. Fleury saw the catechism rather as a "model of instruction" which the priest or teacher would alter and adapt according to the age and background of the learners.

Not everyone was as convinced as the authors of the Tridentine Catechism and Fleury of the need to adapt and accommodate method

5. H. DeLubac, *Catholicism*, New York: New American Library, 1964; p. 169.
6. A. Etchegaray, *Storia della catechesi*. Ancona: Edizioni Paoline, 1965; pp. 275-285.

to audience. In 1761 Pope Clement XIII expressed alarm that "the different ways of teaching Catholic truth have brought about conflicts, rivalry and disunity of minds" *(In Dominico Argo)*. He feared a lack of uniformity had given rise to confusion and scandal. His solution was to have a single, adult catechism "adapted to the understanding of all, even the uneducated." Clement's solution would have been in large part to insure a certain uniformity of language.

The Proliferation of Catechisms in Ireland and Elsewhere

As a nation, the Irish are more aware than most of how language becomes a pawn in the contest for minds and political allegiance. The research that Father Wallace did for his doctoral dissertation illustrates how the English manipulated even the language of the catechism for other than religious purposes. The first book printed in Ireland in the Irish language was Sean O'Kearny's Protestant catechism in 1571. Queen Elizabeth recognized that, if she was to advance her political ambition and promote the reformed church of Ireland, she would have to use the language of the people. (In effect she acknowledged the failure of Henry VIII's programme to uproot the Irish tongue and popery simultaneously.) From Elizabethan times to the decline of Irish as a spoken tongue, a number of Protestant catechisms, printed in the Irish language, circulated among the people.

It was forty years before the Catholics responded in kind with the *O'Heoghusa Catechism* compiled by the Irish Franciscans in Louvain (1611). There followed a series of catechisms, some in Irish for the people, some in Latin and English for use by priests. In the early penal days most were produced abroad and showed in various degrees the influence of Peter Canisius, Cardinal Bellarmine and the Council of Trent.

It was characteristic of these catechisms that they include frequent exhortations to virtuous living, helps toward pious exercises and, like the catechism of St. Peter Canisius, aids to devotion. Doctrine is presented as the basis and nourisher of the spiritual life. Anthony Gearon's *Parrthas an Anma*, for example, is in fact "a Catholic prayer book which enshrines a catechism". The first part describes a day in the life of a Christian.

> He rises to say morning prayer (at an elaborately decorated altar); he attends Mass as though he was present on Calvary. As he works he reflects on the Holy Family in their daily occupations. In his intercourse with the neighbours he respects them, a man as though he was Christ, a woman as though she were Our Lady. After the day's work, he examines his conscience, divests himself

61

of his cloak while reflecting on Christ being stripped of his garments and resolves to rise at midnight for matins...[7]

In addition to presenting faith, hope and charity after the traditional Augustinian manner, Gearon stresses the spiritual implications of doctrine for day to day living.

In Ireland, in addition to the Gaelic catechisms already mentioned, the eighteenth century gave rise to a number of catechisms in English. The work, however, that was to exert a dominant influence in Ireland (and as we shall see in the United States) for close to two centuries, was the manual compiled in 1777 by James Butler II, archbishop of Cashel. It came upon the scene when an Anglo-Irish nationalism was emerging and political concerns began to overshadow religious differences. The Butler catechism was both a reflection and an instrument of the new political movement. Wallace states that "the available evidence indicates that it was....(the) political initiative which let to Butler's catechism being officially revised and declared a 'general catechism for the Kingdom'".[8]

It was not only in Ireland that the number of catechisms continued to proliferate. In France bishops saw it a duty of their pastoral office to provide catechisms adapted to the needs of their flocks. Many eighteenth-century works were vehicles for the promulgation of Jansenist and Gallican positions. Napoleon, in his drive to consolidate all authority in the hands of a central government, tried to bring some order to the situation. In 1806 he imposed a uniform catechism on all the dioceses of the French empire, though one suspects he was motivated more by political ideology than a zeal for the unity of the Catholic faith.

Like their counterparts in France, many bishops in the newly independent United States authored catechisms adapted to the needs of their flocks. John England and John Baptist David compiled catechisms for the diocese of Charleston, South Carolina and Bardstown, Kentucky, respectively. Jean Louis Cheverus introduced an English translation of Fleury's catechism into Boston shortly after being named bishop there in 1812. Frederic Baraga of Marquette wrote a catechism for the Chippewa and Ottawa Indians. St. John Neumann composed a catechism for German immigrants in Philadelphia, and in 1850 John Baptist Purcell imported the Deharbe catechism for the use of the German-speaking Catholics in Cincinnati. A year after he

7. Patrick Wallace, *Irish Catechesis — The Heritage from James Butler II, Archbishop of Cashel 1774-1791*. Ann Arbor: University Microfilms, 1975; pp. 83-84.
8. Ibid., p. 106

had produced his own catechism in 1826, Archbishop Marechal of Baltimore wrote to the Congregation for the Propagation of Faith asking what to do about the increasing number of catechisms in the American dioceses. A call for a standard catechism was an agenda item at the first provincial council of Baltimore in 1829 and at the first plenary council in 1852.[9]

Standardization of Texts

The nineteenth century saw several attempts to stem the proliferation of catechisms and impose some standardization on catechetical texts. More time was spent at the First Vatican Council debating the merits of a uniform catechism than was spent on the question of infallibility. Although it was never implemented, the conciliar fathers approved the scheme *De Parvo Catechismo*, which mandated the compilation of a catechism to be used universally by all children. The issue of a standard catechism for the entire Church was seen as a pastoral question. Bishops who spoke in favour of the draft seemed to think that a uniform catechism would be a great convenience, a bond of unity and a remedy for what many perceived as confusion. Bishops who opposed *De Parvo Catechismo* argued that the real issue was not the catechism but catechesis — the manner of instruction, the need to adapt to local and individual situations, and the competence of the catechists. In its final form the schema ran about 400 words. Other than saying the catechism should be modelled on that of St. Robert Bellarmine, which was in use in Rome, *De Parvo Catechismo* did not address any of the issues raised by the opposition.

The action of the Vatican Council undoubtedly influenced the decision of the Irish bishops at the National Synod in 1875 to call for a "national catechism." The "Maynooth Catechism," another revision of Butler's, was the result. It introduced little that was new other than questions and answers explaining the Immaculate Conception (defined in 1854) and papal infallibility (1870). The American bishops followed suit. In the Third Plenary Council of Baltimore in 1884, they authorized a national catechism for the United States. The principal source for the contents and the structure of the Baltimore Catechism was also Butler.[10]

Bishops were among the earliest critics of both catechisms. Archbishop William Walsh of Dublin (1892) launched a

9. Mary Charles Bryce, *The Role of the Bishops in the Development of Catechesis in the United States*. Washington, DC: The Catholic University of America Press, 1984; pp. 27-65.
10. Bryce, pp. 91-92.

comprehensive criticism of the Maynooth Catechism. He complained that it omitted many matters of practical importance in the fulfillment of Catholic duty; was at times needlessly polemical; contained many explanations which were too complicated and used vocabulary which was too difficult. Similar criticisms were levelled against the Baltimore Catechism.

Few of the complaints about the Maynooth and Baltimore Catechism are original. They echo the criticisms that have been hurled against Catholic catechisms since Peter Canisius first published his in the sixteenth century. Insofar as they are directed at the treatment of specific points, the criticisms are not serious and can be remedied. They do, however, point up the inherent limitations of the genre itself; and seen in their cumulative effect, they are serious indeed. The better the catechism is as a manual of instruction, the more likely it is to take on a life of its own. Instead of serving as a tool — a means to highlight basic tenets of Catholic belief and practice — it becomes as end. Mastery of the catechism text becomes a goal in itself. The "small" catechisms like Maynooth and Baltimore which use the question-answer format seem inevitably to encourage rote memorization. The short, concise answers with their rythmic cadence, especially in the hands of untrained catechists, put greater emphasis on orthophony than orthodoxy. A verbatim recitation of the answers too easily passed for correct understanding. Words and phrases that rang different from catechism answers were considered "offensive to pious ears".

A New Genus of Catechisms

Nor did the mandate of Vatican II to publish a General Catechetical Directory stem the tide of catechisms. Even while the Council was in session the Dutch hierarchy commissioned the now famous catechism for adults,[11] and in the wake of the Council individuals and groups everwhere rushed to incorporate the teachings of Vatican II into catechisms of various sizes and formats. In some cases it meant pouring new wine into old skins; in other cases, it was a matter of bottling the wine before it was ready. While work was going forward on the General Catechetical Directory the Italian hierarchy was carefully laying the groundwork for a new national catechism. It began by issuing a foundational document whose spirit and vision is remarkably similar to the General Directory, and then over a period of years

11. *A New Catechism*. New York: Herder, 1967, See Michael Donnellan, "The German and Dutch Catechisms in Retrospect," *The Living Light* 12 (1975): 20-29.

published a graded catechism adapted for age groups from infants to adults.[12]

Given the origins and history of the catechism it is not surprising that Germans are among its strongest promoters, though they differ among themselves as to the approach modern catechisms should take. Two catechisms which appeared in 1980 illustrate some of the differences: *Botschaft des Glaubens. Ein Katholischer Katechismus*, originally commissioned by the bishops of Augsburg and Essen, is a systematic compendium of doctrine and seems best adapted for use in school. It is a straightforward presentation of Catholic teaching unencumbered with discussion of contemporary issues or life's problems. The other, *Grundriss des Glaubens*, translated into English as *Credo. A Catholic Catechism*, which seems to have taken its inspiration from the model catechism for adults outlined by the late Adolf Exeler, was compiled by members of the German catechetical association and authorized by the commission for textbooks of the German Bishops' Conference. The text strikes a nice balance between instruction and inspiration. It provides a comprehensive overview of Catholic doctrine and moral principles, and builds a Catholic vocabulary by explaining terms and practices. The aim, however, seems more to present the Christian message as a vision, an orientation which influences individuals in making life decisions and commitments.[13]

In light of these publications in Germany and elsewhere, one is puzzled by Cardinal Ratzinger's comment: "It was an initial and grave error to suppress the catechism and to declare obsolete the whole idea of catechisms".[14] It is clear, however, that he did not consider them adequate. Within a year of the publication of the two German works Cardinal Ratzinger, then chairman of the Commission for the Faith of the German Episcopal Conference, assigned the task of compiling a new catechism for adults to Walter Kasper of the Catholic Faculty at the University of Tubingen (who later was the special secretary for the Extraordinary Synod). The appointment injected new life into a project, originally authorized by the Conference of German Bishops

12. See Berard L. Marthaler, "The Renewal of Catechesis in Italy," *Religious Education* 65 (1971): 357-363. John E, MacInnis, "Italy's *Catechism for the Christian Life:* More Than Meets the Eye," *The Living Light* 18 (1981): 334-344.
13. "Forum Katechismus," *Diakonia* 8 (1977): 254-279. See my review in *The Living Light* 21(1985): 270-271.
14. Joseph Ratzinger, "Sources and Transmission of the Faith," *Communio* 10 (1983): 18.
15. Walter Kasper, "The Church's Profession of Faith; On Drafting a New Catholic Catechism for Adults," *Communio* 11 (1984): pp. 57, 29.

in 1976, that was near collapse at the time Kasper took it over. The *Katholischer Erwachsenen-Katechismus* deserves careful study because it provides important insights into the kind of catechism that Cardinal Ratzinger thinks will help rescue catechesis from its present crisis. It may indeed be the kind of work that many of the bishops at the Extraordinary Synod envisaged when they recommended "a catechism or compendium of all Catholic doctrine regarding both faith and morals".

Addressing the German Episcopal Conference in the spring of 1984, a few months before the new catechisms appeared, Kasper described its development and situated it in the history of catechesis. Although he cited the Catechism of the Council of Trent as "the best model" — *mutatis mutandis* — for the undertaking, Kasper acknowledged the emergence of "a new genus of catechism" provided immediate precedents for the new German catechism: the Dutch catechism; the ecumenical *Neues Glaubensbuch* (published in English as the *Common Catechism)*; and the adult catechism issued by the Evangelical (Lutheran) Church in 1975.

The new German work corresponds to the "big" catechism of Luther and Canisius — a catechism for catechists, "those transmitting the faith," rather than for catechumens or students. It is Kasper's position that "many of today's catechists are, practically speaking, still catechumens themselves and they must be 'met' where they are".[16] Thus the new catechism could not avoid "stressing some thought-provoking topics if it is not to by-pass the problems of this target group". A great deal of theological work went into the catechism; "but at all times," Kasper said,

> its compilers made an honest effort to preserve room for differing theological schools and directions within this creed which is binding on all Catholics. In order to keep this free space open, since that is indispensable for the life of the Church, it was impermissible to have this catechism pass prior judgment on any of the numerous, profoundly important, questions in theology which are legitimately and even necessarily, being raised today.[17]

Given the fact that in his closing address, Pope John Paul singled out the proposal for "a compendium of catechism"[18] it is likely to become a reality. If the Synod's recommendation, therefore, leads to

16. Kasper, p. 61.
17. Kasper, p. 63.
18. *Origins. NC Documentary Service*. December 19, 1985. p. 452.

a catechism along the lines of the new German catechism, the apprehension of many will be dispelled. The Synod envisaged

a catechism or compendium of all Catholic doctrine regarding both faith and morals...a point of reference for the catechisms or compendiums that are prepared in the various regions. The presentation of doctine must be biblical and liturgical. It must be sound doctrine suited to the present life of Christians.[19]

The scope of the Synod's recommendation underwent considerable refinement from the raw proposal put forward by Cardinal Bernard Law, Archbishop of Boston, during the first week of the Synod. As summarized in the English Language edition of *L'Osservatore Romano*, he urged that

a Commission of Cardinals to prepare a draft of a Conciliar Catechism to be promulgated by the Holy Father after consulting the bishops of the world. In a shrinking world — a global village — national catechisms will not fill the current need for clear articulation of the Church's faith.[20]

A catechism emanating from such high authority would be a departure from any previous catechism in the Catholic tradition. It would seem inevitable that such a compendium would be given the status of a confessional document like that of Heidelberg and Westminster. In the final redaction, endorsed by Pope John Paul himself, the Synod returned to the idea of national catechisms which would use the new compendium as a point of reference.

The scope of the Synod's recommendation seems to conform more to what Cardinal Ratzinger had been calling for, namely, a comprehensive, organic presentation of Catholic teaching which could be of service in the catechetical ministry. The final proposal of the Synod, moreover, is also quite obviously different from the decree of Vatican I, *De Parvo Catechismo*, which had mandated a "small catechism" for children. As a reference tool the Synod's catechism will be in the tradition of the Catechism of the Council of Trent. Similar to the Tridentine catechism which was for use by preachers and teachers, the compendium proposed by the Synod seems intented primarily for professional catechists and publishers of catechetical materials. Thus the apprehension of many, especially in the English speaking world where the best known paradigms of the catechisms have been Butler and Baltimore, has been greatly reduced.

19. *Origins*, December 19, 1985, p. 448.
20. December 9. 1985; p. 6.

A Precedent

With its emphasis on catechesis for adults and its openness to contemporary issues, the new German catechism conforms substantially to the general principles set down in the General Catechetical Directory. In describing the importance of catechisms the GCD says,

> Their purpose is to provide, under a form that is condensed and practical, the witnesses of revelation and of Christian tradition as well as the chief principles which ought to be useful for catechetical activity, that is, for personal education in faith. The witnesses of tradition should be held in due esteem, and very great care must be taken to avoid presenting as doctrines of the faith special interpretations which are only private opinions or the views of some theological school. The doctrine of the Church must be presented faithfully. (par. 119)

If there is one area in which the German catechism is wanting it is the practical aspect and its lack of suggestions as to how it might be used in catechetical programmes. Kasper justified this deliberate omission by saying, "It is not designed to put didactic expertise in a harness but to set it free." The catechist must be, he said, "allowed the freedom which is necessary for structuring catechesis according as the multidimensional situations require taking into consideration the age, the life-circumstances, the level of formation, and the questions and needs of the catechumens".[21]

The GCD directs that, in presenting the teaching of the Church, catechisms are to follow the norms set forth in chapter one of Part III — from the standpoint of catechesis the most important section in the entire Directory. Beginning with the notion of revelation which, it describes as "the manifestation of the mystery of God and of his saving action in history," the General Directory says it is the task of the Church's prophetic ministry to make the content of this message intelligible so that individuals "may be converted to God through Christ, (and) that they may interpret their whole life in the light of faith" (par. 37). Catechesis must lead to the presentation of "the entire treasure of the Christian message" (par. 38). While emphasizing that the content of the Christian message forms a certain organic whole (par. 39), the Church also recognizes "a certain hierarchy of truths" in which such tenets as found in the ancient creeds are considered basic (par. 43). Catechesis must necessarily be christocentric (par. 40)

---

21. Kasper, p. 69. Cardinal Ratzinger cites the example of the *Roman Catechism*, in arguing that catechisms must allow catechists freedom in presenting the material, *loc. cit.*, p. 33.

and at the same time trinitarian. To neglect the integrity of mystery latent in the phrase "through Christ, to the Father, in the Spirit," is to rob the Christian message of its proper character (par. 41). The Directory cites Vatican I in asserting that one of the conditions required for "a fruitful understanding" of the purpose of the economy of salvation is that the diverse Christian truths be related to human beings' ultimate destiny (par. 42). Although the mystery of salvation "awaits its consummation in the future" catechesis should enable people to understand how it is realized in the past in the incarnation, death and resurrection of Christ, and in the present through the Holy Spirit and the ministry of the Church (par. 44; 45). Despite the fact that there is a definite corpus of material that must be taught, the Directory acknowledges it is not possible to dictate a particular order that must be followed; circumstances must be taken into account in selecting a pedagogical method (par. 46).

In 1983 an outline of Christian Doctrine (Schema Doctrinae Christianae) was presented to and unanimously rejected by the International Catechetical Commission because it seemed so out of step with the norms set down in the General Directory. The Schema, consisting of some eighty articles, was admittedly incomplete. The ICC feared that in its final form the outline would be (mis)represented as a basic catechism which would emphasize neither the organic integrity of the Christian message not the hierarchy of truths.[22] On the other hand, curial officials arguing for endorsement of the schema, went so far as to state that the General Catechetical Directory was outdated and should be substantially revised.[23] It was this incident more than anything that gave the impression that catechetical leaders were polarized, one camp favouring directories, another camp favouring catechisms.

It was against the background of this apparent polarization that many interpreted the action of the Extraordinary Synod. When the bishops recommended a catechism, it seemed to some that they had taken sides and, in effect, ignored the collective wisdom of the Second Vatican Council which had mandated directories. The fact is, however, that Vatican II envisaged both directories and catechisms and, as we have seen above, the General Directory itself provides general norms as well as practical guidelines for the compilation of catechisms. And

22. Wilfrid H. Paradis, "Report on the Fifth Meeting of the International Catechetical Council, Rome, April 11-17, 1983," The Living Light 20 (1984): 167-168.
23. Herman Lombaerts, "Religious Education Today and the Catechism," Mount Oliver Review 1 (1984): 9.

there is Pope John Paul's statement in *Catechesi Tradendae*, which we have already cited, that encourages episcopal conferences "to prepare genuine catechisms... which will be capable of educating the Christian generations of the future to a sturdy faith," in the same article in which he says that the General Catechetical Directory "remains the standard of reference" (art. 50).

No more than the General Catechetical Directory, can a universal catechism or compendium of Church teaching resolve all the problems that beset catechesis. Even after episcopal conferences issue national and regional catechisms, there is still a need to restate the norms and principles of sound catechesis and adapt them to the circumstances of particular cultures, social conditions and age groups. To pose the question as if it were a choice of one or the other betrays ignorance of the nature of the catechetical ministry and dissipates energies. If the recommendation of the Synod were simply an effort to resuscitate the plan of Vatican I, *De Parvo Catechismo*, there would indeed be reason for apprehension because it would mean a return to child-centred catechesis. Interpreted in the context of the General Catechetical Directory, however, the recommendation for a universal catechism is likely to yield a work like the new German catechism for adults. It will be authoritative, but it won't be final. It will build on the precedents of Luther, Canisius, the Council of Trent and, yes, the Dutch Catechism; and if done well, it will be a precedent for future catechisms.

The Catechumen in the Kitchen:
Reflections on Ministry and Catechesis in Ireland

Michael Warren

In this presentation I hope to shed light on some principles that affect catechesis in Ireland and on some affecting religious education.[1] In order to do so, I would like to ground my reflections in an event I participated in the last time I was in Ireland, an event whose significance has come back to me many times.

The event, which took place in the Sandyford area of Dublin, was a Eucharist whose participants were all unemployed men and women in their early 20s, most of whom were on the dole. As you might suspect, since this class of persons is widely known to be alienated from the Church, there was a history to their coming together, and it is important that I explain it. A woman in their neighbourhood had been paying attention to these young people and the way they spent so much time aimlessly on the streets. She noticed in them an edgy disgruntledness and frustration that took bizarre forms of behaviour: drinking to excess, vandalism, and even violence against one another.

She took a further step in her interest by getting to know these young people through casual conversation. She did not have any unsolicited advice for them, but simply took an interest in them as persons and paid attention to what they paid attention to. She listened, tried to understand, gave advice when asked. There was a fair amount of trouble among them, and some of it they brought to her for help, usually when things reached a crisis point. She was occasionally called on when there was family trouble, trouble with the law, or when someone went on a drinking or drug binge. Eventually, a small group

1. I wish to acknowledge the valuable assistance given in the preparation of this essay by Brendan Fay of Drogheda, graduate assistant in the Theology Department, St. John's University, Jamaica, New York.
2. The particular compassion John Paul II has shown to unemployed young people is worth noting, as well as the way he connects unemployment with injustice. See John Paul II, "Speech to Youth," Memorial University, Newfoundland, Canada, 12 September 1984. *Canadian Catholic Review* 2:9 (October 1984): 345-346.

began to meet once a week in her home to discuss their frustrations, both social and personal. They met for months, and the group grew. Drugs, unemployment, boy-girl relationships, marriage, trouble with the law — all these came up during those months, and almost always without any explicit reference to religious matters. It seemed to have been assumed by them that their faith had nothing to do with any of these questions.

Eventually, however, these young people directed their attention to Geraldine, the woman who had been giving them her attention for so many months. She was not married; she had a job with the government, and a comfortable living. Why did she give them her attention and time when she could be occupied with matters less stressful than their problems? And so it was that she came to speak about herself and the religious commitments at the core of her life, which led her to be concerned about these young people without any hidden agenda about getting them to practice their faith. They were intrigued and for a couple of weeks they had questions about the Church and about various aspects of their own childhood faith that made no sense to them. They began to start each weekly meeting with a short reading from scripture and a discussion of what it meant, and to end each meeting with prayer for the ones among them most in trouble.

To make a long story longer, eventually they (none of them Mass-goers) decided they wanted to celebrate the Eucharist together. It might have been a year and a half since they had first started to meet, but eventually, there in Geraldine's home the Eucharist they did celebrate, with a priest who had joined in their discussions from time to time. Though all had been to Mass before, for many it was the very first time they celebrated the Eucharist. And so the night when I was there was one of those times every month or two when they broke bread and passed the cup to remember that in Jesus the Father had turned injustice inside out.

But this story I have just recounted for you of how the whole thing had come about, I myself learned only afterward. I had been invited that night to share in a home Mass with a group of young people. All I knew was that they were older and that they were not of the privileged classes. Looking back now, I see I was not ready for most of it. I was not ready to be squeezed into a small living room with more than fifty young people. I was not ready for the quality of the care they showed for one another, in their awareness of one another's pain, combined with a lack of self-pity. I was not ready for the highly colourful, earthy language they used to express themselves. I was especially not ready for their insights into the meaning of the scripture

readings for their own lives, insights juxtaposed with silence that got deeper and deeper as the reflection continued. Having been invited to a home Mass with some young people, I was not expecting all this. I was surprised and delighted.

I hope the event I have been describing does not sound pious and warm and wonderful, because it was not. There was a tone of very real anger, both at the social situation they were in and at the Church. Their social anger made a great deal of sense to me. Here were young people, young and vital, capable of work and clearly eager to work, showing their bitter scorn for the dole, both the fact of the dole and the meagre size of it. Among the group were couples who wanted to marry but who judged they could not, for lack of a living wage. They wanted to get on with their lives and with their loves, to have homes and children, and to have the financial basis necessary for life together. However, it was lacking to them.

I have thought many times afterwards what it must mean to have no place, to be told you have no place in your own land, the country of your birth. You are excess baggage. We do not need you. Not only do you have no contribution to make to the social project, you are an actual burden on that project. What must it seem to these young people, to have energy and eagerness to work and to be told you have no place, even before you have had a chance to prove yourself?

To find an example from Irish history that illumines the injustice of this situation, one would have to go back to the time of the famine and look at certain proposals the British overlords had for the starving peasants.

> The idea that the peasantry had become superfluous in Ireland, that more attention should henceforth be given to ridding the land of people and stocking it with cattle, gained more and more adherents among Ireland's landlords as the famine's ravages continued. It was an idea set forth repeatedly by Lord Carlisle during his visits to Ireland, in words like these: "Here we find, in the soil and climate, the condition best suited for pasture; hence it appears that cattle, above all things, seem to be the most appropriate stock for Ireland.... Corn.... can be brought from one country to another from a great distance, at rather small freights. It is not so with cattle, hence the great hives of industry in England and Scotland can draw their shiploads of corn from more southern climates, but they must have a constant dependence on Ireland for an abundant supply of meat."

> Great Britain wanted a pastoral country nearby to produce meat for its industrial workers, and since a pastoral country could not be a populous one if its flocks and herds were not to be

eaten at home, the Irish people were being told, by way of evictions and the pulling down of cabins, to clear out of Ireland.[3]

As all here understand, there was no place in Ireland for its own people at the time of the famine. What does it mean today for its young people to face the prospect of never in their lifetimes having a permanent job? What does it mean to be young and to be told in various behavioural ways that you should think twice about marrying and having a family, because you will spend your life not knowing from one day to the next where the next meal is coming from?

I began to see that, in this religious place and at this holy event, their social anger was religious. Citing Chrysostom, Aquinas notes that "he who is not angry when there is cause for anger, sins."[4] In this sense we can speak of the virtue of anger and claim that "a lack of anger in certain situations means a lack of willed commitment to the good of justice."[5] I wish these young people had known how much on their side was Church teaching, as found for example in the three principles set forth by the Bishops of Canada in a recent pastoral on economic justice.

1. The basic rights of working people take priority over the maximization of profits and the accumulation of machines.
2. In a given economic order, the needs of the poor take priority over the wants of the rich.
3. In effect, the participation of the marginalized takes precedence over an order that excludes them.[6]

However, as I have already indicated, their anger in that Eucharist was also directed against the Church or at least against a particular understanding of the Church. They seemed convinced that the Church had taken sides and sided with the well-to-do and not with them. Though nobody cited particular policies favouring the children of the

---

3. Thomas Gallagher, *Paddy's Lament: Ireland 1846-1847* (NY: Harcourt Brace Jovanovich, 1982), pp. 145-146. I make this analogy with considerable trepidation since my lack of background in Irish history could lead to easy distortions. Such a danger has been brought home to me by: Michael O'Higgins, "The Tyranny of Images,"*The Crane Bag* 8:2 (1984): 132-142.

4. Cited in Daniel Maguire, "The Primacy of Justice in Moral Theology," *Horizons* 10:1 (Spring, 1983): 72-85, at 78.

5. Ibid.

6. Canadian Conference of Catholics Bishops, *Ethical Choices and Political Challenges:* Ethical Reflections on the Future of Canada's Socio-Economic Order (Ottawa: Concacan Inc., 1984), pp. 5-6.

wealthy over the children of the poor, still this conviction was strong. I was especially intrigued with what I will call their catechetical anger, which scoffed several times at various teachings learned when younger but which now seemed ridiculous. I cannot remember the specific points ridiculed, but they all seemed to be the hortatory teachings, the oughts and the musts. Freely assembled around bread and wine, engaged in intense discussion of Jesus' place in their lives, these young people had the wit to make these disembodied "thou shalts" seem ridiculous indeed.

Catechesis in the Framework of Ministry

Eventually I came to see in this Eucharist and in the events leading up to it some important aspects of ministry and of the relation of catechesis to pastoral ministry. I realize, of course, that there are some who might question whether a Eucharist with Dubliners on the dole has any catechetical significance at all. I presume there are still those who limit catechesis to instruction in doctrinal formulations and who tend to see it as something that passes between teachers and students in classrooms. I, however, prefer to view catechesis within pastoral ministry, rather than with education. As a form of the ministry of the word, catechesis cannot function properly unless it is integrated into a total work of the Church that includes the three other ministries: the ministry of worship, the ministry of guidance and counsel and the ministry of healing. In ministry there is a kind of balance of nature, a symbiosis, with the various forms in harmony with one another.[7] What happened in Sandyford illustrates this point well.

It is worth noting that in her approach to these young people, Geraldine did not do catechesis at all. There was no explicit religious message. She instead took the stance of guide or counsellor and of healer. In other words she did what she did because it was part of her integrity as this kind of Christian person. She might not have named it as such, but her work with these young people comprised two of the four fundamental aspects of ministry; the ministry of guidance and counsel and ministry of healing. Both these ministries are action-oriented but rooted in the primal action of noticing, of listening, of trying to discern. It is the ministry of those who are wise enough to be literally dumb. If they will know we are Christians by our love, one of the sure signs of love is attentiveness.

Perhaps we could call these two basic ministries: guidance/counsel

---

7. See, "Youth Ministry in Transition," Chapter 1 of M. Warren, *Youth and the Future of the Church* (Minneapolis: Winston-Seabury, 1985), pp. 8-16.

and healing, the ministries of credibility. At least for those who stand outside the circle of faith, these are the works that make the community's life believable. They cannot be feigned, because they either make the good news seem like good news or they do not. It was when these young people realized that Geraldine herself was good news to them, that they inquired about the sources of her good news. And it was when they inquired that she gave them an account of the faith that was in her. She had at that point moved into the ministry of the word, which is a ministry of accountability, in the sense that it gives an account of the roots of one's action. These young people knew that she did not love them as potential church-goers because she had not proposed church attendance to them. She loved them because they glowed with the goodness of God. Geraldine did not want to bring them to God. What made the difference (I suspect) to these young people is that Geraldine had already found God present in them.

I have gone into this in some detail, because Geraldine's work with these youth exemplifies so well the work of evangelization.[8] Because evangelization is an aspect of the ministry of the word, its chief form might seem to be the verbal, but its foundation is in deeds; and those deeds begin not so much in an attempt to influence another as in an attempt to be true to one's call to discipleship. The first form of evangelization is not a verbal announcement at all, but a commitment to justice and to solidarity with the oppressed, to the point of being with them in their efforts to have their injustices redressed.[9] Another way to say it is that Geraldine did not begin by "talking the way" with these young people but by "walking the way" with them. Eventually the whole process reached the point of words, talk about the realities of Christian faith. Gradually those who presumed those realities meant nothing to them came to judge that they meant everything to them. When they came to see that they stood inside the circle of faith or wanted to stand there they had crossed over into the zone of catechesis, which always presumes faith. From there they proceeded to worship, which itself continued their catechesis because it was in the context of worship that they struggled to understand

8. For an overview of the centrality of evangelization in contemporary catechetical thinking, see, M. Warren, "Evangelization: A Catechetical Concern," in Warren, ed., *Sourcebook for Modern Catechetics* (Winona: St. Mary Press, 1983), pp. 329-338.

9. An important treatment of this key aspect of evangelization is: Jon Sobrino, "Evangelization as Mission of the Church," Chapter 9 of *The True Church and the Poor* (NY: Orbis, 1984), pp. 253-301.

further what faith was calling them to, what it meant to them.

Catechesis and worship, then, were not the first steps in the journey at Sandyford; they were final but continuing steps. Geraldine presumed little (except the possibilities) and started where the young people were; together they took a kind of exodus journey out of alienation to the Eucharist. I would like to stress, however, that this journey was one they entered into themselves and then progressed in a step at a time. They were not marched along to an alien beat like prisoners of war. Evangelization and catechesis can only take place in an ambience of freedom and choice.

Two Irish catechetical dilemmas

If you have followed carefully my story of ministry in Sandyford you have seen in it special problems for the Roman Catholic Church in Ireland. I would like to set out briefly two of them as meriting further attention.

First of all, the Church in its ministries of credibility needs to be present *on the side* of the most disadvantaged or marginalized in Ireland. If the Church in its organized life had been on the side of these young people, it was not apparent to them, nor was it apparent to Geraldine. Among the followers of Jesus, systemic unemployment which denies any persons their fundamental human rights must not be met with either the silence of words or the silence of deeds. The teaching Church in Ireland has well pointed out that the horrors of Latin America at root stem from economic inequities, with the haves in the position of privilege and power, not willing to give an inch of their comforts, and the have-nots being in a position of desperation. Possibly the same teaching needs to be applied to Ireland, geographically far removed from Guatemala and El Salvador, but morally much closer than we might like to admit.[10] "Quite recent research has shown that while the top 10% of Irish households have 42% of the income, the bottom 19% have little more than 4% — the biggest inequality in the EEC."[11]

10. According to Peadar Kirby, many working for justice in Ireland have made the same comparison. See Peadar Kirby, *Is Irish Catholicism Dying?* (Dublin: Mercier Press, 1984), p. 90.
11. John McGrath, SSC, cited in Denis Carroll, "The Option for the Poor," *The Furrow* 33:11 (November 1982): 672. Another way of stating the same inequality is: "The top 20% of Irish income earners take in 43.4% of all income earned; while the bottom 40% receive only 15.7% of all income earned in the country." Peter McVerry, "A House Divided," *New Creation*, (August 1982): 27.

I stress this point because at issue here are catechetical matters in several layers. If there are structural inequities present in Irish society, then colluding in them are managerial-class and investment-class persons who name themselves as followers of Jesus and on whom has been lavished the best talent and the best facilities the Church has to offer.[12] These persons have a special responsibility to be on the side of the have-nots, though they may not all have heard the gospel preached as good news about justice. Even further, could it be that adult catechesis in general has been ignored in Ireland. Have catechetical leaders fully accepted the fact that the days are gone when Christian faith could be passed on through family traditions and through socialization in village or neigbourhood values? In the age of television, could it be that expressions of robust faith like the following hymn of Peig Sayers can only be continued through deliberate nurturing, which will need careful catechesis?

> My love my Lord God! Isn't it straight and smooth life goes on according to His true holy will! Shouldn't we be joyful for His glorious light to be lit amongst us! Isn't there still many a person lying in the dark! God with us, Lord, isn't that a pity! I understand that there is no more valuable jewel in life than to have love for God of Glory... for I see a lot that reminds me of the great power of God.[13]

As lovely as this hymn is, to be appropriate to our time, the second sentence may need a corrective to point out how evil systems can spin on, smoothly countering every aspect of God's will.

The second dilemma hidden in my tale of Sandyford is one of finding the proper relationship between catechesis and ministry. In its ministry, the Church, while on the side of the victims must also be *at* their side, as a guiding, healing presence among the people. Establishing such a presence may be a particular problem in Catholic Ireland where some might expect certain of the Church's ministries to be institutionalized in services provided by the state. I realize that I am alluding here to a large theoretical question that needs careful analysis. Still, the parish that gives the impression that its one and only ministry is that of

---

12. There are, of course, two sides to collusion in unjust systems. The poor can also collude when they do not take seriously their own need to participate in the formulation of social policies. See, Richard Quinn, "Economic Development and Christian Faith," *The Furrow* 35:4 (May 1984): 306-318.
13. Peig Sayers, *An Old Woman's Reflections* Tr. Seamus Ennis (NY: Oxford University Press, 1972), p. 29. See Higgins, "Tyranny of Images," pp. 139-142.

worship has already begun to die, because it has ignored its wider mission.

A good example of a ministry that can function properly only in the local believing community is the ministry of catechesis. As an ecclesial activity, catechesis cannot, of its very nature, be relegated to the schools. The *General Catechetical Directory* makes clear that the chief catechizer is not a teacher, even one called a catechist, but the believing community itself.

> Within the scope of pastoral activity, catechesis is the term to be used for that form of ecclesial action which leads both communities and individual members of the faithful to maturity of faith. With the aid of catechesis, communities of Christians acquire a more profound living knowledge of God and of his plan of salvation centred in Christ.[14]

Notice the communal stress here. Catechesis is not for children only; in fact it is not even mainly for children. It is primarily adult activity, that is, a lifelong struggle to make sense of death, evil, injustice, and suffering, a struggle that emerges with something to celebrate.

If catechesis is mainly done apart from the local community of faith and mainly in schools, what happens to a young person who leaves school at age fifteen or sixteen? Is that person, who is apt statistically to be from the poorest sectors of society,[15] to live the rest of his/her life with a primary school understanding of faith? Are there not understandings of faith appropriate or even accessible only at later moments of life, including some of the more complex issues of justice and peace? Who then will be the catechist for this fifteen year old no longer in school? Or who for example will catechize the business executive in Howth, whose decisions may worsen economic injustice in Ireland?[16] If the local Church does not face up to catechesis as its own work, then we leave our people with the "catechesis of the tube," with the catechesis of *Dallas* and *Kojak*, a religion geared to the ever greater fulfillment of consumer fantasies. We no longer have a choice

---

14. Sacred Congregation for the Clergy, *General Catechetical Directory* (Washington: USCC, 1971) Par. 21, p. 21.
15. The statistical evidence for this claim can be found in "Aspects of the Education and Employment of Young People in Ireland," Chapter 8 of, *National Youth Policy Committee: Final Report* (Dublin: National Stationery Office, 1984), pp. 73-93.
16. A nuanced presentation of the need for adult catechetical work in Ireland, though not stressing the justice perspective, is, Liam Lacey, "Adult Catechesis in Ireland: A Way Forward," *The Irish Catechist* 7:3 (October 1983): 31-41,

in this matter. We either, like the Third World Churches, ground our work of religious transformation in slow and careful catechetical ministry or we abandon our people to oppressive systems, in this case to the marketeers.

If the abundantly researched erosion of faith in Ireland is a symptom of the lack of adult catechesis,[17] then possibly that symptom will begin to disappear when more persons trained at Mater Dei begin to take their places as fulltime pastoral assistants providing catechetical leadership in parishes. Not every priest is a good catechist, just as not every priest is a good preacher. Some who preach poorly are wonderful counsellors; others are gifted at works of compassion and healing. Above all, a priest in our day is called to be the affirmer and nurturer of the gifts present in the community. When gifts are thus nurtured, then we will find those who are to be the presence of our community at the sides of the alienated, the way Geraldine was for the young people at Sandyford.

Perhaps the possibilities of a broader approach to ministry in local parishes can be illustrated with what a young man told me one night in a pub in Maynooth. He had left the seminary and was then studying at St. Patrick's College. He said something like this:

> If I went to my bishop and told him that I was thinking I might have a vocation to be a priest and that I was willing to begin studies for the priesthood, I would get every sort of openhanded encouragement. If I didn't have the means, I would receive financial help. My summer employment would be aided, partly because I was studying to be a priest, partly because I had good connections through the Church. I could go and be ordained; and yet a year after ordination I could throw the whole thing over and go sell insurance.
>
> However, if I went to my bishop and told him that I had been in the Young Christian Students and Young Christian Workers since I was fifteen, and that I had been spending almost twenty hours a week working to develop a Christian understanding among the unemployed in Dublin; and that I was finishing a degree in religion at St. Patrick's College and wanted to undertake a fulltime ministry with young people in the Church, I would receive the bishop's good wishes and no more.

He also claimed that the bishop was likely to tell him that he should become a teacher. He was quite clear however that he did not wish to serve in that structure.

17. For an overview, see, Liam Ryan, "Faith Under Survey," *The Furrow* 34:1 (January 1983): 3-15.

I have stressed here the catechetical importance of the Church's being on the side of the most marginalized and of placing catechesis within ministry. In this concluding section, I wish to comment explicitly on the role of the school in dealing with religious understandings. To be blunt, I have great doubts about the possibilities of catechesis in the schools. In my view, schools should be doing religious education and leaving catechesis to be done by and within the local church community. There needs to be an extended discussion of this matter here, such as is currently underway in the U.S. and Canada.[18] I suggest the following three points be included in that discussion.

1.   A fundamental question, often overlooked by teachers but basic to understanding the social reality of a school, is the following: Under what circumstances and auspices do those who assemble in schools come together there? And what sort of institution is it in which they assemble? I would love to believe, as one whose profession involves teaching in a school, that the young who assemble there do so willingly because of my skill as a performing artist and because of the luminous quality of my reflections. Yet I know students do not assemble in a university for the reasons people assemble in a theatre. The forces in the university are complex and even contradictory.

In a primary or secondary school, however, the forces are much more direct and compulsory. Those who assemble in those places do so because not to do so would mean the intervention of the state in their lives. Since civil law mandates schooling up to a certain age, those who assemble in schools do not do so out of a full choice on their part. To admit this fact is not to deny that many children and youth actually enjoy various aspects of life at school. In fact, Irish youth rank teachers at the top of the list of those who understand them, just after parents, a wonderful tribute to the teaching profession.[19] Still, the primary and secondary school does not exist as a zone of full choice, as becomes clear when we contrast the school with the worshipping community.

The worshipping community is meant to be the place of free assembly. Why? Because it is in the nature of human beings that celebration can only be proposed; it can never be imposed. At the moment of imposition, celebration ceases to be true celebration and

18. See, James Dunning, "Words of the Word: Evangelization, Catechesis, and the Catechumenate," (Washington: North American Forum on the Catechumenate, 1984).
19. *National Youth Policy Committee: Final Report*, p. 54

becomes something else. It might superficially look like celebration but the heart has been cut out of it. Celebration works from the inside out; compulsion works from the outside and never fully gets in. Not all in the Church like to face the implications of this fact, i.e., that obligation subverts the act of worship.[20]

Catechesis is a cousin of celebration. In the early Church, full catechesis could only take place after the ecstasy of both having gone down into the water of baptism and shared in the broken bread of the body. This fullest form of catechesis was mystagogic catechesis, a pondering of the wonderful things that had happened.[21] Mystagogic catechesis was the final step in the catechumenate, a process every step of which the community insisted be free.

If freedom and choice is a central aspect of catechesis, then that aspect is masked somewhat when catechesis is done in the zone of obligatory attendance, i.e., the school. In catechesis the person is actively pursuing his or her own understanding. The catechist presumes that the person has already embraced Jesus' way and stands inside the circle of faith. In a school that presumption of choice is not so possible as it was, say in Sandyford. Everyone at the Eucharist in Geraldine's parlour was there actively seeking an enrichment of his/her faith life. What was interesting to me was that not every person was in the parlour. In the kitchen was a young man who had decided he could not celebrate the Eucharist until he had stopped his compulsive and destructive drinking. How he came to that decision I have no idea, but all understood and accepted that he was not fully ready. So all the time we were there at the Eucharist we were aware that there in the kitchen was someone not fully ready, our "catechumen," who was a full member of the group through friendship but whose lifestyle needed more work before sharing the cup.[22] That incident illustrates for me the choices so central to catechesis, but not necessarily central to a school.

2. Religious education, on the other hand, falls not within ministry

---

20. See, Josef Pieper, *In Tune with the World: A Theory of Festivity* (Chicago: Franciscan Herald Press, 1973)

21. An excellent account of mystagogic catechesis can be found in Hugh M. Riley, *Christian Initiation*, Vol. 17 of Studies in Christian Antiquity, Johannes Quasten, ed., (Washington: Catholic University of America Press, 1974).

22. The importance of change of lifestyle in the early catechumenate was highlighted by Regis Duffy, OFM, "Liturgical Catechesis: Catechumenal Models," The First Annual Mary Charles Bryce Lecture. Washington, Catholic University of America, 1983.

as does catechesis, nor is it a cousin to celebration.[23] It rather falls within education and involves, not a way of walking like catechesis but a way of studying. It is a kind of inquiry and is more similar to the study of science and literature than it is to catechesis. If I could play with my words "impose" and "propose," I am not even sure one can propose literature. The study of literature is a process of exposing it rather than proposing it, that is, of looking at the history of various literary forms and of the ideas and emotions contained in them. To be educated does not mean having come to adopt any of those forms oneself but to understand them as part of the legacy of human expression. The possibility of such understanding is of course itself a great gift.

Similarly, religious education is also a great gift, which examines religious questions, including christian ones, not so much from the point of commitment, which is the perspective of catechesis, but from that of intellectual inquiry.[24] What seems especially important about religious studies or religious education in Ireland is that it can dispel multiple illusions young people can develop about religious matters: that the religious is limited to the christian; that the religious is something imposed on them by an institution called the Church, rather than an area of human achievement pursued in all cultures of all time; that other religious forms are "wrong" in the face of our "right" way. Religious education seeks religious literacy, that is, a broad understanding about how religious forms work, especially about how religious language works.[25]

In doing religious education, we need not exclude the examination of Christian and Roman Catholic matters, but we examine them from a much more objective stance than that used in catechesis. Catechesis presumes conversion; religious education presumes some willingness for disciplined inquiry. Its goal is not growth in commitment so much

---

23. An attempt to compare and contrast catechesis and religious education is, M. Warren, "Catechesis: An Enriching Category for Religious Education," *Sourcebook*, pp. 379-394.
24. See, Michael Grimmitt, *What Can I Do In R.E.?* (Great Wakering: Mayhew-McCrimmon, 1973), esp., Chapter 5, "A Conceptual Framework for Religious Education in Schools," pp. 49-87.
    Contrast Grimmitt's treatment with the jumbled categories used in the following news report, Christina Murphy, "Education is secular, says teacher priest," *Irish Times* (26 June 1982): 15. Another essay lacking in my view conceptual clarity is: W. Richard Maher, "Religious Education and Schools — a Perspective," *The Furrow*, 36:1 (January 1985): 27-36.
25. See, for example, Grimmitt's treatment of this matter. Ibid., pp. 59-75.

as growth in understanding. The fulfillment of catechesis is worship and action for justice. The fulfillment of religious education is mastery in an intellectual sense.[26] I claim that such an approach to religion is especially important after about age 14-15, when many young people need a chance to re-think religious questions from new standpoints and in doing so actually re-think their own religious commitments.

One of the reasons I stress the value of religious education is my commitment to catechesis. We will never move to religious education until catechesis is more properly situated in the local Church, as a lifetime pursuit of fidelity to discipleship. The pursuit of fidelity certainly has its ups and downs, which is one reason we have a sacrament of reconciliation at all. If we knew that the catechesis necessary for a lifelong pursuit of discipleship was going on in our local churches, we would then be able to broaden our approach to religious matters in schools, where intellectual inquiry is the appropriate mode. However, where there is little lifelong catechesis going on, I can see how persons in the schools might be reluctant to move toward religious education.

3. A further aspect of schools deserves a word: the issue of freedom. If Christian faith cannot be imposed, neither can education, because in its deepest sense education also comes from inside out. A key problem schools have to grapple with is that of establishing a consensual climate. When a person reaches the age for secondary school there must be sensitive attention to the establishment of such a climate. In schools there is an educational triangle among whose parts must be developed a harmonious balance: the faculty, the students, and the subject matter.[27] The relation among these parts needs to be

26. Still deserving close attention is the following treatment of the religious studies question in third level education, Cosmas Rubencamp, "Theology as a Humanistic Discipline," in George Devine, ed., *Theology in Revolution* (NY: Alba House, 1970, pp. 185-197.

27. "A major concern of this Committee has been the provision of opportunities for young people to participate in their society. To this end, we asked young people if they see it as important that they be involved in the decision making procedures of their schools and colleges. The vast majority (82%) felt they should, and the suggestions received particular support among the under 17's and those still in school. Young people in urban areas, and females, also saw this as being particularly important." *Youth Policy Committee: Final Report*, p. 84.

See also, Theodore Sizer, "A Study of High Schools: A Proposal" (Washington: National Association of Secondary School Principals, March 1981). Another version of Sizer's proposal is found in his more recent book, *Horace's Compromise* (Boston: Haughton, Miffin Co., 1984), pp. 154-171 and 205-213.

negotiated between students and teachers. One does not establish consensus by incessantly asking students,"What would you like to do today." Yet if students have not agreed to a particular line of disciplined inquiry, there will be little learning. In modern societies with ready access to information via television, young people are more and more resisting the imposition of education forms in which they have no say.

Not having visited schools in Ireland, I have no firsthand knowledge of how they are run. From descriptions of educational events in Irish literature, one finds inklings suggesting consensus receive more attention. I found another inkling recently in an essay by Louis McRedmond in the London *Tablet*. Writing about the nasty behaviour of "La Thatcher" at the Anglo-Irish Summit in the fall of 1984, when she insulted both the Irish Prime Minister and the work of the New Ireland Forum, McRedmond used an analogy suggesting volumes about the way she sees education in Ireland. He wrote, "She looked and sounded the stern headmistress, rejecting an unreasonable petition from the fourth form. As the headmistress would do, she offered a brief explanation in simple terms suited to childish minds. Each option, she said, would involve a diminution of British sovereignty. This was unacceptable because the majority of the people of Northern Ireland wanted to remain British. Class dismissed.... This forum had not been a caucus of schoolchildren."[28] One hopes this analogy comes from McRedmond's remembrance of schools past, and is not true of schools today. Fourth formers, even when being unreasonable, need a more gracious and understanding reception than the supercilious response of this headmistress. The fact of the matter is that La Thatcher's response would also have been insulting to the fourth form. At all levels of education, dialogue is the appropriate form, not communiques from on high. Communiques undermine education, though they are the death of catechesis. In dealing with religious issues, schools need to be especially open places.

Conclusion

In this presentation I have tried to illustrate one approach to catechetical method. Instead of beginning with a discussion of theoretical matters, I chose to begin with a concrete incident focusing attention on the marginals in our society. I did so out of a conviction that the option for youth should be fused with the option for the poor. If our entire programme of ministry, including catechesis, begins

28. Louis McRedmond, "Anger in Ireland," *The Tablet* (1 December 1984): 1192.

among the marginals, at their side and on their side, that position provides us with the radical questions for discipleship in our time. As for issues, I started with unemployment because it is a catechetical issue. To deny that it is, is to bring catechesis back to the worst caricature of its true nature, and alas, the one that prevailed for so many centuries, i.e., catechesis as a doctrinal message mainly conceptual and moralizing but cut off from any deep concern for the contours of the lives of the hearers. Unemployment *is* a catechetical issue. The key catechetical documents for our time are the social justice documents. It is a mistake to separate the economic aspects of our lives from the doctrinal and ethical, because the separation takes place in one's head only. At the level of living, they will always be related. I have also chosen as seminal the image of the catechumen in the kitchen, because it highlights the catechetical questions of choice and readiness. It also draws attention to the life-giving but tolerant posture of those who gather in faith, who are secure enough in their own continuing search for fidelity to allow time and space for the one who does not quite fit. Irish kitchens have been the places that for eons have welcomed openhandedly the wanderer, and perhaps they symbolize the warmth offered by a people sensitive to the marginal and displaced because they themselves as a people have been marginalized and victimized.[29] I have come here to remind you of the catechetical significance of that tradition.

29. See, Diarmuid O Laoghaire, SJ, "Old Ireland and Her Spirituality," in, Robert McNally, ed., *In Old Ireland* (NY: Fordham University Press, 1965), pp. 46-47; also, *Paddy's Lament*, p. 14.

Moral Development: friend or foe of Christian Education?

Gabriel Moran

The question raised in the title of this essay is whether twentieth century theories of development and historical Christianity go in the same direction. Some of these ideas are worked out in further detail in my book, *Religious Education Development*.[1] However, I am not trying to summarize that book. My focus here is more directly on morality. I will argue that development can be a helpful idea if it is first freed from its captivity by economists and one school of psychology. I will then make a case for the compatibility of modern education and of a traditional wisdom that the Church embodies, sketching the main lines of a developmental scheme for education in Christian life.

I am to a large extent arguing with two people who have exercised considerable influence in church circles: Lawrence Kohlberg and James Fowler. Kohlberg on moral development and Fowler on faith development have affected textbooks and curricula of religious education throughout the English speaking world. Kohlberg is the larger adversary; his influence has been much greater, spreading out over two decades.[2] For reasons that I will indicate, I think that his theory of moral development is at odds with a Christian education.

James Fowler's work became well known only with the 1981 publication of his *Stages of Faith*.[3] Although often mentioned in the same breath with Kohlberg, Fowler attempts to offer a corrective to Kohlberg. In talking about faith as developmental, Fowler is trying to make a direct contribution to the Christian work of education. For over a decade, I have had a friendly and respectful disagreement with

1. Gabriel Moran, *Religious Education Development* (Minneapolis, Winston Press, 1983).
2. See Lawrence Kohlberg, *The Philosophy of Moral Development*(San Francisco, Harper and Row, 1981); *The Psychology of Moral Development* (San Francisco, Harper and Row, 1984).
3. James Fowler, *Stages of Faith* (San Francisco, Harper and Row, 1981).

him. In his recent book, *Becoming Adult, Becoming Christian*.[4] Fowler has a response to my criticism. I have to say that his response is not really concerned with my fundamental point of disagreement which is about the nature of development itself. Despite our differences, I am not disparaging his work which is of considerable value to Christian educators. I think that precise and respectful disagreement is what education should entail.

A survey of the literature on moral development — heavily influenced by Kohlberg — reveals that moral development is assumed to begin about the age of six and continue until the late teens. Moral development is conceived to be mainly a mental progression, sharpened by the discussion of hypothetical dilemmas. From the perspective of much of the world's culture and nearly all religions, this description of morality is remarkably narrow. But once the word development has been defined as a psychological or epistemological category, then criticism from a political or religious basis simply does not penetrate the system of ideas called moral development.

In the twentieth century, moral development has been closely associated with moral education. A concern for the questions of moral education sparked interest in a theory of how people develop morally. If there was to be hope for success in the rational project called moral education, there had to be some structure of personal life which reasonable men could appeal to. If everyone does in fact move through the same sequence of life stages, then education has the well defined task of designing instruments to aid the advance.

Moral education, as the term has been used in this century, can be traced to two main sources: Emile Durkheim and Jean Piaget. The work of these two men is usually seen to be opposites, with Piaget concentrating on "mental operations" and Durkheim interested in the socialization process. Durkheim's work came first in his 1901 book, *Moral Education*.[5] There he appealed for a rational morality to be inculcated by society through its schools. Piaget's 1932 book, *The Moral Judgment of the Child*,[6] describes the epistemological changes which issue in distinct moralities at different ages. Piaget's book is also an attack on Durkheim for his reliance on "authority" and for making school-teachers a new priesthood of that authority.

Although differing in many respects, Piaget and Durkheim were in

4. James Fowler, *Becoming Adult, Becoming Christian* (San Francisco, Harper and Row, 1984).
5. Emile Durkheim, *Moral Education* (New York, Free Press, 1973).
6. Jean Piaget, *The Moral Judgement of the Child* (New York, Collier, 1962).

agreement on one major point. Both believed that Christianity is a great obstacle to moral education. Their search was for a moral stability and moral progress unencumbered by dogmatism and intolerance. Christanity was thought to be at best a pedestrian sort of morality based on fear or at worst an immoral burden on human shoulders. Therefore, from its twentieth century beginning moral education/moral development has excluded religion on principle. The idea of development has functioned as a secular substitute for providence, predestination and heaven. That is, development is what lures us on to something bigger and better even though there is no guiding hand to the movement nor any endpoint to the process.

Surprisingly little is written on the idea of development itself. Or perhaps it is not surprising that a notion so central to a whole era is simply taken for granted. Development is a term that shows in almost every field of study today. It is one of those optimistic modern words that nearly everyone wants a share of. Its two closest relations are progress and evolution; but development avoids the presumptuous connotations of the former and the biological limitations of the latter. At the same time, development can function as a term that comprehends individual and cultural change. And in a more muted way than the word progress, development still suggests a change that is for the better. Thus, the issue of *moral* development is not peripheral to development because to move from a worse to a better stage implies standards by which to measure good, better, best.

The two groups of people who most frequently use the term development are psychologists and economists. Each group is almost totally oblivious to the use of the term by the other group and ostensibly there is no direct connection between the psychological and economic meanings. However, I think that some underlying connection between the two usages is an intriguing possibility that deserves exploration.

The field of 'development psychology' tends to assume that it invented the idea of development. Psychology departments offer courses presumptuously called 'human development'. Psychologists thus imply that not only psychological development by human, personal, moral, religious developments are to be discovered and described by psychology. But it is not at all clear in scholarly and popular contexts that development is the preserve of psychologists. Indeed, one might suspect that psychology came rather late to the idea of development and that psychology does not today hold controlling interest in the term.

I have said that the other sphere where development reigns is economics. Michael Novak makes the claim that development is an idea invented by Adam Smith in 1776.[7] In Smith's *Wealth of Nations* there is the idea that one can indefinitely expand wealth by the organization and investment of resources. The process which is guided "as if by an invisible hand" has no endpoint but is nonetheless a bettering of the human condition.

Even if one does not assign the credit to one man at one moment of history, Novak and others interested in economics would seem to have a good case for tracing the idea of development to the economic revolution at the beginning of modern times. Phrased differently, economics arose as part of the rise of modernity, progress and development. In that perspective, "developmental psychology" is an application of the idea of development. The application to psychological data may be appropriate but one should not forget a larger context of meaning for development.

When we come to "moral development" there is no obvious reason why it should be seen as belonging to psychological development. But in the last fifty years since the publication of Piaget's book on moral judgment in children, more development has increasingly been defined as a psychological, epistemological or "cognitive" question. The name of Lawrence Kohlberg has become almost synonymus with moral development. When Kohlberg is pressed, he admits that he cannot measure moral development; he claims to measure stages or moral reasoning. I would say that more precisely he measures stages of reasoning about hypothetical moral dilemmas. Although Kohlberg acknowledges that the link between this scale of measurement and other categories of moral activity is at best unclear (and at worst non-existent), both he and his followers slip into talking of their work as one of measuring moral development.

I would argue that moral development should be related to all the fields that use the word development. In ways that may not be easily measurable, moral development may be related to physical, social, political, religious and other kinds of development. And, of course, economics being so central to development, one must ask about the correlation of moral development and economic development. To ask about this relation may seem to be a silly question but perhaps it is just an embarrassing one.

The nineteenth century was not adverse to drawing a direct correlation between moral progress and wealth. At the end of the nineteenth century, many Christian churchmen joined this chorus. One famous preacher said bluntly what many people only suggest:

---

7.   Adam Smith, *Wealth of Nations*, (1776).

"No man in this country suffers from poverty unless it be more than his own fault — unless it be his sin."[8] In 1901 the Rt. Rev. William Lawrence addressed the issue in an essay, "The Relation of Wealth to Morals". Expressing no doubt about the direct and positive relation, Lawrence wrote: "In the long run, it is only to the man of morality that wealth comes. We believe in the harmony of God's universe. ... Only by working along the lines of right thinking and right living can the secrets and wealth of Nature be revealed. We, like the Psalmist, occasionally see the wicked prosper, but only occasionally."[9]

Many Christian writers today, particularly in Latin America, are inclined to turn Lawrence's picture upside down. Based on the Jesus of the synoptic gospels, a negative correlation between moral development and wealth would seem more defensible. My intention is not to propound such a thesis; I am not addressing the question of the Christian view of poverty. My main concern is the narrowing of the idea of moral development.

Wealth or lack of it is a much too narrow foundation for measuring development. The concern with economic development can be at the expense of social, political, aesthetic, cultural and religious forms of development. The wealthy nations have taught everyone to refer to the developed and the developing worlds. The language is illogical and insulting. All nations are developing nations and those with great wealth do not necessarily offer a model of development for others. From the 1950s to the present the United States has explicitly tried to sell its idea of development to Latin American countries.[10] It has to a large extent succeeded. But for anyone brought up in the United States it is a shock to discover Latin American writing that views the U.S. as developmentally retarded. When we move away from measurement in dollars, it is not all clear who should be called the "third world", a phrase appropriated by people who were sure they were first and second.

The economic meaning of development tends to engulf every other meaning of the term, including the psychological. Economics supplies the controlling image for the direction of development. This image is so all-pervasive in U.S. culture that we hardly notice it as an image at all. I refer to the image of growth. Development as applied to the

8. Quoted in Henry May, *Protestant Churches and Industrial America* (New York: Harper, 1967), p. 69.
9. William Lawrence, "The Relation of Wealth to Morals", in *God's New Israel*, ed. Conrad Cherry(Englewood Cliffs: Prentice Hall, 1971). p. 246.
10. Comblin, *The Church and the National Security State*.

person had to be a quasi-religious movement to replace providence, predestination and heaven. The unlimited potential of the individual was to be freed from the shackles of the old gods and old dogmas. One had to get rid of any end point to the journey or else "man" would not be truly free. Growth without limit was the way to stipulate direction and to avoid closure to the process.

John Dewey's educational writing was often attacked for being vague and mystifying on the issue of growth. But Dewey knew just what he was doing; he was simply ahead of the full flowering of the term development in both economics and psychology. Dewey's progressive education could have been called growth education. "There is nothing that education is subject to save growth", wrote Dewey, "and nothing that growth is subject to save more growth."[11] Later critics, like Richard Hofstadter or Boyd Bode, wanted to know: growth in what?[12] It was not that Dewey had somehow neglected this question. He knew that in questions of "objectives" one had to say growth in knowledge or growth in employable skills, but as for education itself or for human development, the direction has no end point and can only be described as growth in growth.

John Dewey was slightly ahead of his time on this meaning of development. When he started writing in the late nineteenth century the economic scene was still one of individual entrepreneurs and small companies. Individuals amassed fortunes and companies sought to turn a profit. There was still a sense of limit to all of the business dealing. The modern corporation dates from only about 1890. The legal control on the corporation was overwhelmed by the spread of the national corporation and then the trans-national corporation.[13] This new phenomenon often seemed illogical by the old standard of selling goods and making a profit. By 1971, John Kenneth Galbraith could write: "The modern corporation is a form of association whose fundamental impetus is to grow. ... Growth is its basic orientation, continued growth without any purpose or end beyond sheer growth."[14] As Dewey had foreseen, growth in profits, plants or products cannot be the endpoint; growth in growth is what provides a quasi-religious exhiliration to life.

11. John Dewey, *Democracy and Education*, p. 51.
12. Hofstadter, *Anti-Intellectualism in America*, p. 373; Boyd Bode, *Progressive Education at the Crossroads* (New York: Newson and Co., 1938) p. 83.
13. Ralph Nader *et al. Taming the Giant Corporation* (New York: Norton, 1976).
14. John Kenneth Galbraith, *The New Industrial State* (Boston: Houghton, Mifflin, 1967), p. 257.

At the psychological end of development's meaning, the words "growth and development" often function as a single phrase. The fact that the two words are joined by "and" suggests there are two different referents. In practice, there seems to be only one thing referred to by the phrase. A case can be made that early in the century growth and development were parallel and related movements, one physical and one psychological. Nothing is more evident about young children than the physical growth of the organism. When developmental psychology was clearly a form of child psychology, development as a psychological process was seen to be at least partially dependent on physical growth. The child's mental capacities would generally have a better chance of developing in a healthily growing body. Piaget called himself a "genetic epistemologist", that is, someone whose interest was the organic basis of rational thought.

In recent decades there has been interest in adult development or life-long development. Such notions cannot really be tacked on to the the previous developmental psychology. Development throughout adult life requires a rethinking of the way psychology had been using development. But a frank reappraisal of the term's meaning has not been undertaken. Instead, adult development and lifelong development were attractive phrases to which no one was likely to object. The one bridge from the old to the new was the cultural favourite: growth.

In the popular psychology that spread throughout the U.S. in the 1950s and 1960s no word is more prominent than growth. As Dewey had foreshadowed, the interest was not growth in knowledge, love, commitment, efficiency, but "human potential", the call to growth without restriction.

Barbara Ehrenreich's *The Hearts of Men* is a provocative history of "growth psychology" in relation to both feminism and economics.[15] Ehrenreich begins her story with the first issue of *Playboy* magazine. In her interpretation, *Playboy* was an economic revolt on the part of men who resented carrying the burden of the family's expenses. The first article in the first issue is by Hugh Hefner on the economic injustice done to men by the system. Anyone who complained about the economic system of the family in the 1950s might have been accused of being gay and/or communist. *Playboy* cleverly avoided those suspicions. It celebrated capitalism and consumer buying. And an interest in pictures of unclad women protected the reader against the suspicion of being gay.

15. Barbara Ehrenreich, *The Hearts of Men* (Garden City: Anchor, 1983).

The Playboy philosophy, as Hefner styled it, was only one piece of the economic and psychological puzzle. The same plea for male liberation began to emerge in novels, popular psychology and social movements. "Growth psychology" flowed throughout the 1960s, supplying approval for many of the longings and rebellious feelings that had been present for decades. Ehrenreich sees Betty Friedan's 1963 book, *The Feminine Mystique*, as a response to men's demanding liberation from their economic and psychological fetters. Citing Abraham Maslow's growth psychology, Friedan asked: "What happens if human growth is considered antagonistic to femininity, to fulfillment as a woman, to woman's sexuality?" Friedan's answer was that it would be unhealthy. Men and women would both have to grow as much and as fast as they could. "The Human Potential Movement saw the growth impulse as so powerful and compelling that it could only be resisted by willful repression. Thus, to deny growth was worse than lazy, it was a perverse and destructive expenditure of energy in the service of an obsolete emotion — guilt."[16]

While much of U.S. culture is still obsessed with the image of growth, there are some points of resistance. When the resistance is simply reactionary, the problem is further obscured. For example, a pro-family movement that fails to address issues of contemporary feminism provides no solid ground for the family. A back to nature movement that celebrates organic growth over technology can actually worsen the hegemony of the growth image. A religious movement that defends "traditional values" can still bring such things as U.S. expansionism into its catalogue of virtues.

At other places in the culture one can hope that a serious and effective criticism of "development as growth" is occurring. Feminism is not the preserve of upper class U.S. women. There is worldwide concern with the shifting relations of women and men. The personal development of both sexes is bringing about some new forms of partnership rather than a competition to see who can outgrow whom. Economically, a central concern of feminism is how women's lives are affected by economic systems. Western style development in its obsession with growth is often deleterious to women.[17]

Ecology presents the most direct challenge to the dominance of growth. At its best, ecology is not a romanticizing of nature but a

16. *Ibid.*, pp. 96-7.
17. See Irene Tinker, "The Adverse Impact of Development on Women", in *Women and World Development*, ed. Irene Tinker, M.B. Bransen and M. Buvinic (New York: Praeger, 1976)

scientific understanding of the complex relations needed for life on earth. In their brilliant book, *The Liberation of Life*, Charles Birch and John Cobb elaborate in detail a picture of a world where growth is not the controlling image. From an ecological point of view, Dewey's "growth is subject to nothing but growth" is insane. "What we can be sure about is that nothing grows forever because the environment has a limited carrying capacity for living organisms."[18]

A world wide interest in spirituality and religion should also lead to resisting the idol of growth. While some of U.S. spirituality is a selling of supergrowth to t.v. audiences, there is also in the U.S. and around the world a search for deeper values. Religion has traditionally provided people with rituals and codes that encourage hope, awaken responsibility and support people in their moral activity. Religion is not likely to imagine moral development as indefinite expansion. Religion can be dangerously irrational at times and it needs the challenge of rational criticism. Nonetheless, religion still offers a powerful resistance to philosophic or scientific claims to understand fully "human development".

Where religion is most helpful is not in having a secret knowledge of some further stage of moral development. Religion for the most part is a simple and concrete reminder concerning the path to moral perfection. In various symbolic ways it says: This is not God, that is not God. The Quran tells its followers: "Toward God is thy limit". A direction to life is specified but one is warned not to expect God as the object of one's quest. The absence of an endpoint leads to "conversion", a return to oneself and a reconsideration of whether one's plan of moral progress makes sense.

The word conversion has been misused by fundamentalist groups so that it is imagined to be a vertical entrance of God or a human leap above reason. Conversion as a circling back on oneself and the recapitulating of life at a deeper level are needed images in the movement of moral development. At least some of the religious meaning of conversion is needed to provide development with an alternative to either unlimited growth or an endpoint, both of which ultimately destroy the idea of development. For moral development we need a movement of responding that deepens the personal centre of response while broadening the base to which response is made. Instead of a single, dramatic point of conversion, the responsible life is one lived in continual conversion, an idea that does not preclude there being one or several times in life that are experienced as particularly formative.

18. Birch and Cobb, *The Liberation of Life*, p. 38.

Religion often speaks of a 'new man' after conversion, a claim that is easily dismissed by moral philosophers, psychologists and social scientists. Of course, in the most literal sense, the claim is false; no one totally abandons her or his previous history. Eventually, one must find an integrity of life, an acceptance of what one is ashamed of as well as what one is proud of. Nevertheless, the language associated with dramatic revelatory insight and courageous decision is a reminder that human beings are capable of surprising even themselves. People are sometimes able to marshall extraordinary moral virture and, alas, the surprise can go the other way. People who have a reputation for moral strength can fail badly when heroism is required.

In summary, it is quite common for Christian writers to set the ideas of development and conversion in opposition. Forcing a choice between the two or placing one above the other is not only unnecessary but is destructive of both. Development has to be movement in the direction of harmony, integrity and never ending fulfillment. It needs the imagery of a constant circling back and down, an integrating of a sphere around its centre. Likewise, the religious idea of conversion needs the idea of lifelong development lest it become irrational in its identifying isolated events and words as God's. Life in conversionary development moves toward a mysterious integrating of divine and human. The individual human being becomes willing to sacrifice the self that is possessed for the sake of a self that is beyond human imagination but intimated in the great moments of ecstasy, love, care, sorrow and bereavement.

Ages/Stages of Moral Development

I make no attempt here to duplicate Kohlberg's three levels and six stages of moral reasoning. However, a few comments can be made about major parts of the moral journey. A main point I wish to make is the close relation between age and stage, a position in contrast to Kohlberg's charting of progress from stages one to six.

As the years have gone by, Kohlberg has become more sceptical about the mass of people getting to the post-conventional level of stages five and six. Starting from a somewhat optimistic expectation that at least ten percent of the population could get to the very top, Kohlberg began to doubt that anybody except a few of history's great heroes ever get there. But whether anyone gets to the top or not, Kohlberg's focus remained on scoring tests and classifying people along the road of clear moral reasoning. Age plays a role insofar as one could not start reasoning about moral dilemmas until age five or six years; and by the end of adolescence one has developed the capacity to reason almost as far as it will go. Kohlberg belatedly came to acknowledge that the experiences of adult life seem to be a necessary condition for exercising advanced moral reasoning. Moral stages in Kohlberg's system remain ways of thought that can be charted in the minds of "school age" youngsters.[19]

In the moral development and moral education described here, the stages have names like infancy, childhood, young adulthood, middle age, elderhood. Everyone goes through all the stages in the course of a lifetime. While it is doubtless possible for a person not to arrive at elderhood's integrity, there is no reason to assume that most people do not. And it would be arrogant to pronounce with certainty that a particular individual has utterly failed. Moral categories, such as integrity, admit of degree. Some people's lives shine brightly for the rest of us, many struggle along a meandering path, and some people's lives appear to be a tragic failure. But there is a final ironic twist in all such moral judgements. The New Testament and other religious documents warn us that the people who are moral failures are not the obvious sinners who are condemned by their fellow human beings. Real failure involves processes of self-deception, a topic I will come back to shortly.

My description of moral development does leave a distinction between age and stage. One gets to each age of life merely be staying alive. One gets to each stage of moral development by responding to what life offers at every age. Thus, everyone gets to every stage and through every stage but not equally well. Education is what fills the gap between age and stage. Education as a re-shaping of life forms is a moral quest to see that each age is better. If development is to be lifelong, then obviously education has to be lifelong in more ways than just a little adult education being added to children's schooling. Moral development occurs through family care of small children, disciplined play, instruction in a discipline of knowledge, the reform of the economic world of work, the intimacy of friendship, political debate and the quiet moments of contemplative thought.

Whatever is good education is moral education. The principle may seem to be a mere tautology but people often assume a wide gap between moral education and the rest of education. A discussion of moral dilemmas can be a helpful means of moral education for one age in one setting. However, moral education extends to whatever truly deserves the name education. Thus, moral education begins at

19. Lawrence Kohlberg and Edward Fenton, "The Cognitive Developmental Approach to Moral Education". *Social Education*, 40(April, 1976). pp. 213-16.

birth, if not before: it continues throughout life in the symbolic articulation of physical, communal activity.

Moral development is centered on personal response set within a matrix of relations. If one tries to describe moral development in infancy one cannot avoid referring to the moral development of parents and grandparents. The "parenting" of a child is one of life's great adventures and so is the 'childing' of one's parents by every infant. The responses of infants and parents are not equal but that fact does not exclude the beginnings of mutuality. Strangely enough, it is the relation between the very young and the very old, often embodied in grandchild/grandparent, that does approach an equality in receptivity.

Our era may go down in history as the time when the deep bond between the very young and the very old was discovered or rediscovered. Their bond of vulnerability is a chief litmus test for the rest of society intent on productivity, control and self-realization. No greater help can be given to the very young than genuine human care for the old. "A society which does not provide sufficient gratifications for the elderly will be an unhappy society for the young as well as the old. If the old are not gratified, nobody can accept the prospects of age with equanimity."[20]

Moral development for the very young consists mainly in what is received as a gift. The modern secular world does not know what to do with this fact which fits neither teleological nor deontological systems of ethics. It seems grossly unfair that at life's crucial beginning the individual whose life is in question has no control. All he or she can do is respond. Of course, in a religious view that sees all creation as a gift, the small child becomes a revelation of the human condition rather than an exception to the ''normal'' situation when individuals control their own destiny. The attempt to exclude religion in modern ethics not only eliminates dogmatic systems and rigid moral codes but also the sense of gift and gratitude at the centre of life.

A receptive attitude on the part of the very young makes possible a little later the acceptance of external guidance. Indispensable to moral development is a commitment not only to a code of conduct but to disciplines of work and study. Most people who have been recipients of generous and affectionate care may have occasional conflicts with a moral code but they do not experience it as a terrible daily ordeal. Behaving according to civil standards is offered as a token return for

---

20. Robert Katz, "Jewish Values: Sociopsychological Perspectives on Aging", in *Toward a Theology of Aging*, ed. Seward Hiltner(New York: Human Sciences Press, 1975), p. 141.

all that parents, society and culture have freely provided. Learning to observe and to understand rules of conduct is an important part of moral development in the period of about five to thirteen years of age. Piaget's concentration on that period, together with his definition of morality as rules and the individual's respsonse to rules, wildly overestimates the significance of reasoning and rules in moral development. However, to Piaget's credit, he did sense that when the child came to perceive that the rules do not in fact add up to a just world, then another universe of discourse would have to take over.[21] Lawrence Kohlberg, in contrast, did not seem to sense the severe and inherent limitation of investigating how children reason about moral codes.

Even in the lives of children and teenagers, reasoning about rules is not the centrepiece of their moral development. When William James was asked how he would increase the "ethical efficiency" of the school, he answered: "I should increase enormously the amount of manual or 'motor' training relative to the book work, and not let the latter preponderate till the age of 15 or 16."[22] In the context of recent discussions of moral development James's reply would strike many people as bewilderingly irrelevant. But placed in the context of the profound issues raised by feminism, ecology and religion, James's answer does not seem so strange. He is calling attention to the fact that morality is at bottom a bodily response to a community's way of life. Ethical thinking will be vacuous unless it is reflection from within the matrix of well developed relations.

The physical training of young men is indispensable to moral development. Boys have traditionally had open to them a wide range of physical work and sports programmes. As for young women, many new opportunities in work and sports have recently opened. The U.S. government's Title Nine, which guarantees equality in school athletics for girls, was a step forward in moral as well as physical development. Feminist writers as early as Mary Wollstonecraft in 1792 had seen the importance of physical training for women.[23] It took a long time for the government to see the point and even now there are danger signs of backsliding in the government's interpretation of financial equality. The corner has probably been turned in the past ten years and women's athletic programmes are not likely to disappear. What remains is to

21. Piaget, *The Moral Judgment of the Child*, p. 323.
22. Quoted in Michael Sadler, *Moral Instruction and Training in the Schools* (New York: Longmans, Green and Co., 1908), p. 94.
23. Mary Wollstonecraft, *The Rights of Woman* (New York: Dutton, 1929), pp.; 23-57.

see that all boys and girls, not just a privileged elite of talented athletes, have opportunities for exercise, sport and physical training.

Physical development need not be at the expense of study, as James's words seem to suggest. The doctrine of "a sound mind in a sound body" of an earlier era was not far off the mark. The prototype of the relation need not be college football programmes with their cynical attitude toward study. There is no inherent reason why physical training programmes in general should not help a young person's studies. Likewise, work-study programmes can enhance the academic life. In some specific areas of study, for example, social studies or languages, experience "in the field" may be necessary for fruitful study.

A whole-hearted response to life is the moral issue for the young. The response includes the physical, mental, social, spiritual and vocational. If their elders do not always approve the particular forms of that response, let the elders voice their concerns and criticisms without undercutting or souring the sense of youthful response. The young cannot give up their selfishness if they have not yet achieved a sense of self. They need encouragement to commit themselves to the particulars in life — some one or some few people who can be cared for and loved, some thing or a few things that awaken a vocation to work. As R.S. Peters notes: "To get a boy committed to some worthwhile activity such as chemistry or engineering, is no less part of his moral education than dampening down his selfishness."[24]

Here is where religion can trip over itself precisely because it has something so important to offer to morality. Christianity is often thought of as a religion for youth. Adolescence as a distinct age in life arose in part as a time when one would undergo conversion. The seventeenth century Puritans had thought that conversion could occur as early as age eight.[25] The enlightened nineteenth century recognized that "loyalty to Christ" could not be achieved before the teen years.[26] What should have become apparent in the twentieth century is that the ultimate challenges to selfhood in the Christian gospel are chiefly aimed at middle age. There are few things so dangerous as mature judgments adopted by immature minds. Religions that preach selflessness to young people can be an obstacle to moral development.

24. Richard S. Peters, "Concrete Principles and the Rational Passions", in *Moral Education*. Five Lectures (Cambridge: Harvard University, 1970), p. 40.
25. Morgan, *The Puritan family*, citing Cotton Mather, *A Token for the Children of New England*(Boston, 1700).
26. Kett, *Rites of Passage*, p. 204.

Conversion, as pointed out earlier, is not a one time leap at age eight, eighteen or eighty-eight. It is a word to denote the recurring movement of return to self in its deeper relations. Of the many conversionary movements throughout life, it is at midlife that one is most likely to encounter the extreme paradoxes of the Christian gospel. Only at midlife is one faced with the decision of letting go of a self that has been acquired.

There seems to be some significant differences between men and women on this point. Midlife crises as a dramatic "de-illusioning" of life have, until now, been mainly a male affair.[27] Women's crises have not been so concentrated; they have begun earlier and have spread throughout the middle years. Perhaps middle age conversion will come to be more similar in women's and men's lives. Or physical and social differences may continue to dictate the crises at different times and in a different rhythm. In either case, the conversionary movements of middle adulthood are central to moral development that is not closed to religion.

If middle age is the time for radical reorientation in moral development, old age is a time for solidifying one's gains. When one arrives in old age, serious illnesses have usually been encountered, parents and friends have died, children are beyond direct control. For the first time since childhood a very simple moral attitude becomes possible. One is grateful for what has been and contented with the day's lot. Despite harsh social conditions (often unnecessary) and declining physical strength, many people report that old age is one of the happier parts of their life. Paul Claudel might not be so unusual for writing at the age of eighty: "Some sigh for yesterday! Some for tomorrow! But you must reach old age before you can understand the meaning, the splendid, absolute, unchallengeable, irreplaceable meaning of the word 'today'."[28]

Younger adults often see the old as grasping at time while the years roll by faster and faster. No doubt there are older people who feel that they are running out of time. Such a feeling is what Erikson calls despair, the flight from death because it means the end of the world.[29] But those who have lived as responding selves continue to be rooted in bodiliness, time and community not because these things are immune to death but because they put us in touch with a deeper

27. Daniel Levinson, *The Seasons of a Man's Life* (New York: Knopf, 1978, p. 193.
28. Katz, "Jewish Values: Sociopsychological Perspectives on Aging", p. 146.
29. Erik Erikson, *Childhood and Society*, 2nd ed. (New York: Norton, 1963), p. 269.

sense of life. Abraham Heschel in his older years wrote: "He who lives with a sense for the presence knows that to get older does not mean to lose time but rather to gain time."[30] The dreams of the old are not just memories of the past but deeper appreciation of the present.

Deep rootedness in the present is the only trustworthy place for visions of the future. The vision of the young in this society is likely to move in a straight line toward family, career and other goals. In old age the lines do not move that way. Neither a teleological nor a deontological ethic has much to say to old age. Responsibility, however, remains a vital category right up to a person's last breath. We need settings which encourage and support that responsibility in two particular ways: sharing with the young and serving those who are more in need than themselves. There is some danger of romanticizing the wisdom of the elderly as if they suddenly become speculative philosophers at age seventy. The wisdom of the old lies more in their attitude of quiet receptiveness and their provision of memory to the young. There is also some danger of creating a second childhood in caring for the elderly whereas many of them need a challenge to do whatever they can in serving the needs of others.[31] Study, prayer and physical presence are possible in any age as resistances to the human temptation toward self-centredness and self-pity.

30. Abraham Heschel, "The Older Person and the Family in the Perspective of Jewish Tradition", in *Aging and the Human Spirit*, ed. Carol LeFevre and Perry LeFevre (Chicago: Exploration Press, 1981), p. 42.
31. Arthur Fleming, White House Conference on Aging, 1971 as cited in Eugene Bianchi, *Aging as a Spiritual Journey* (New York: Crossroad, 1982), p. 161.

PART THREE
Charting the Way Forward

PART THREE
Charting the Way Forward

Religious Education: A focus for the future

Una M O'Neill

The critical questions that face Religious Educators today are well known. They include the growing religious apathy and indifference of young people; the urgent need to establish consistency and continuity between what is taught in the schools and what is experienced in the parishes; the whole question of education for peace and justice; the need for an inclusive spirituality; the vital question of Religious Education as an integrated ministry shared in partnership between home, parish and school. The list is long and the problems are great. All of them impinge on our consciousness and each deserves time and attention.

Even so, I have chosen not to address them. My choice arises from a conviction deeply held. My conviction is that it is time for us to pause; to develop a self-awareness that is born from reflection on the experience of Religious Education over the past twenty years or so; to spend some time in that contemplative form of knowledge from which alone can emerge deeper insights and new visions of understanding that will enable us to move into the future with conviction and enthusiasm. The real foundational need is to re-root Religious Education in a solid self-awareness that arises from such reflection.

Such an approach is not easy and not attractive. It is much more interesting, more attractive, more satisfying, at least in the short-term, to deal with those aspects of the enterprise that affect us directly and concretely: to offer programmes of action rather than to ask people to reflect on the depth or superficiality of the theological, educational and psychological foundations of present programmes.

If we don't pause, however, and spend time in this reflective activity, then we are in danger of engaging in one of two equally fruitless, even harmful, activities. We will either fall into the trap of thinking we can solve our problems by formulating a framework that is really nothing more than a synthesis of elements from present theory and practice that appear on the surface to have relevance for the present, or we will try to resuscitate a framework that is already dead.

We have to face the fact that the future of Religious Education can only, and must only emerge creatively from the process of attending to the issues as they have emerged from past and present tradition, and, from that attending, to protect a future direction that is realistic in terms of present experience, faithful in terms of the past and solidly creative in terms of the future. Otherwise we may think that the way forward is to develop a rash of new programmes, write a wealth of new textbooks or wear people thin on activities that have a shortlived affective result.

This lengthy introduction to the theme I have chosen has an addendum.

Apart from my conviction as to the importance of the theme there is a second reason for addressing it. These talks are dedicated to Fr. Pat Wallace and when I think of his contribution to the field of Religious Education I think of tension: the tension of being true to the past while being open to the future. People who can live creatively with this tension are the truly great educators, and Fr. Wallace is one of these. Most of the rest of us continually spend our time bemoaning the present, regretting the past or denying its validity, fearing the future or exhausting it by that frenzied anticipation that destroys its promise. Religious Educators like Pat Wallace save us from this destructive waste of energy by the singleminded conviction and enthusiasm with which they engage in the field.

Our reflections on Religious Education might start by generalizing on some of the experiences that have affected it from the turn of the century and before. These experiences include the shifts of focus which arose from the growing appreciation of historical consciousness and the demands of critical enquiry, both of which gained impetus from the broadening of the philosophy of human knowing and understanding. Equally significant for Religious Education were the historical and scientific insights that steadily eroded the image of a fixed and stable interpretation of the universe and our experience of it. Likewise, the science of communications had ploughed through geographical boundaries and intensified our awareness of the existence of profound cultural and historical differences between peoples.

Of equal importance in latter years has been a shift from the static conception of knowledge to an understanding of knowing as progressive and a realization that truth is not a possession that can be subjected to disinterested analysis but is involved in the process of history.

Aware of the significance of these and other factors for the person's experience of God, faith, and religious meaning, Religious Education turned its attention on the one hand, to its roots in the theological

106

analysis of the intrinsic relationship between revelation, faith and contemporary human experience, and, on the other, to its educational rootedness in the contemporary sciences of psychology, sociology and education theory.

At the practical end, this issued in a real attempt to relate religious experience to life experience; to devise child and adult programmes and textbooks that respected and endorsed that relationship; to create liturgical experiences that called for involvement, for variety in prayer, for varied ministries; to initiate social experience and praxis that called for conscientization on issues of injustice, powerlessness, underprivilege, denial of human rights.

The main question that has directed this experiential focus has been: "How can we offer people an inspiring vision of faith that will lead to an authentic christian life?" and Religious Educators have struggled, often in isolation and frustration, to discover ways of bringing people to maturity of faith; ways that they considered meaningful, relevant and directly related to the reality of living in the 70's and 80's.

The movement has been good. Sometimes we are inclined to lose sight of the distance travelled, the amount achieved. Religious Education has, in these past years, tried and generally succeeded, in overcoming the negativity and naive fideism that some forms of Religious Education encouraged in the past and has challenged individuals and communities at the level of meaning, identity and christian praxis.

The movement in Religious Education it must also be said, has been one of great commitment on the part of those engaged in the field that has often been frustrated by lack of leadership. It has been a movement of growth towards christian community that is rooted in the paschal mystery of Christ that has been frequently frustrated by lack of real opportunity. It has been a movement of people willing to serve the Kingdom-cause of justice and peace that has often been unfairly judged as naive, irresponsible and even anti-ecclesial.

At the academic level, Religious Education in the past years has been backed by theological considerations of the relationship between authority and experience, faith and rationality, historicity and tradition, meaning and truth, experience and revelation, faith and the secular. This theological reflection has served, on the one hand, to root Religious Education solidly in its christological and revelational foundations. On the other hand, it would have to be said, that some of the theological discussion concerning Religious Education has become an end in itself and done little to further the practical realization of living faith in the 1980's.

Furthermore, and more disconcertingly, the creative reflection and reinterpretation which is essential to any genuine faithful theology, and which theologians can generally engage in with a measure of freedom, has at times rebounded negatively and constrictively on Religious Education. Afraid of the ill effects of such creative theology on the people of God, those charged with the care of Religious Education have manifested an unease that has served, on occasion, to further entrench and solidify reactionary positions in relation to religious education and its objectives.

If we reflect on the past therefore, we can see that there has been considerable growth in the field of Religious Education, genuine success in its efforts to reach and teach people of our day, more committed involvement by lay people, a deeper understanding of its aims and objectives. At the same time one would have to acknowledge from this reflection that we have now reached a stage where we are in danger of being overwhelmed by the various concerns that face Religious Education, some of which were outlined at the beginning of this paper. If we try to meet these concerns too easily, we may deny their root causes in a frantic effort to shore up our faltering enthusiasm.

So, before we can look for a positive way forward we must reflect first, not only on our past but on our present experience and try to discover the foundational cause which is giving rise to the problems which Religious Education is encountering with increasing frequency and strength.

Such reflection very quickly surfaces an aspect of our present-day experience which is having increasingly negative repercussions on the religious consciousness of people in our day. It is an experience which can be described as functional in the negative sense and which is beginning to dominate our secular experience. Increasingly, it is spilling over into the religious experience of people in a harmful and destructive way.

I am using the word 'functional' in a specifically negative sense, recognizing that there is a functional interpretation of reality that is good and necessary. When I talk of functionalism therefore I am speaking of an approach to reality that trivializes human experience and tranquillizes the human urge to self-transcendence. It is an approach that exalts the pragmatic and relegates the theoretic to the sphere of the impractical; that believes only in truth that is objective and verifiable at the empirical level; that promotes our self-imprisonment in power and possessions and mocks the spirit of selflessness; that defines success in terms of measurable achievement alone; that describes the creative imagination as unreliable, arbitrary, irresponsible, escapist, unreal.

The effects of this functionalist approach to reality are easily recognizable. I will mention a few.

Functionalism paralyzes the urge to reflective questioning and so prevents the move to a self-conscious appropriation of experience. Heidegger describes it as

> This downward plunge into and within the groundlessness of the inauthentic Being of the 'they', has a kind of motion which constantly tears the understanding away from the projecting of authentic possibilities and into the tranquillized supposition that it possesses everything or that everything is within its reach.[1]

It exalts the technological imagination and downplays the poetic. This is described with some bewilderment in John Hewitt's lines

> Do all men wait like this for breaking light or, tired of waiting turn to stem the time with jerking gestures and a swab of words, till grown to numbness, they are content at last to accept the twitching nerves and the stung lids.[2]

Similarly, functionalism militates against an attitude of openness and wonder towards our experience of reality which is essentially human. Such an attitude makes life a discovery and not a boring endurance, every answer the basis of a new question. A functionalist approach smothers this wonder. Bernard Lonergan describes it as an attitude of 'complacent inertia', the result of the person's smothering of the desire to know.[3]

Truth, understood functionally, is valued only if it can be understood and measured empirically. People are persuaded to substitute the passion for life and love with the passion for power and possessions. Substitutes for passion are of course provided when all else fails and these engage our energies in order to deliver us from guilt. Such substitute experience is described rather wickedly by Michael Hartnett in the following lines:

> . . . we chose to learn the noble art of writing forms in triplicate. With big wide eyes and childish smiles quivering on our lips we entered the Irish paradise of files and paper-clips.[4]

In the world of functionalism the criterion of value is usefulness. If the immediate and practical value of something is not perceived, then it is of no use.

As I have described it, functionalism results in a flatness of

1. Martin Heidegger, *Being and Time* (Oxford:Blackwell), trans. 1980, p. 223
2. John Hewitt, "Expectancy", *The Selected John Hewitt*, Blackstaff Press, 1981, p.116.
3. Bernard Lonergan, *Insight* (London:Longman, Greene & Co.), 1967, p. 348.
4. Michael Hartnett, "A Farewell to English", *Collected Poems*, vol. 1 (Dublin: Raven Arts Press), 1984, p. 160.

experience, a dull and passive attitude to life, a suspicious and selfish motivation, a disregard for the depth dimension of life, an inability to sustain reflection and wonder, an approach to people that equates them with their functions and values them only on that basis.

It is fairly obvious that the atmosphere, attitudes and values engendered by functionalism are alien to those which emerge from the religious consciousness of people and which Religious Education seeks to mediate and communicate. More significantly, functionalism erodes, smothers and subdues those basic human experiences in which the question of God arises, and in and through which God reveals himself to us.

Furthermore, it would seem that some of the negative symptoms and questions that have arisen in recent experience of Religious Education have emerged precisely from Religious Education's genuine concern to be relevant to experience but in its efforts to be relevant Religious Education itself has, to some degree, become infected by functionalism.

Indications of this religious functionalism are apparent in school curricula and methodology that insist that one can only teach from within the actual, lived experience of students. Again it is evident in an approach to religious and moral education that defines success solely or largely in immediate, observable, measurable results. It is likewise to be seen in the increasing flatness of the language of Religious Education, a growing use of functional language that is uneasy in the company of art, poetry, mystery and symbol.

Functionalism in Religious Education is reflected in a cosmetic approach to issues of peace and justice that is not sustained in the face of long-term demands or the dreary, humdrum effort. It can be seen in a spirituality caricatured somewhat by Harvey Cox as a "unilateral retreat from the kneeling to the lotus position",[5] or indeed described more poignantly in the following lines:

> . . . prayer in this green island is tarnished with stale breath, worn smooth and characterless as an old flagstone, trafficked with journeys no longer credible to lost destinations.[6]

Finally, religious functionalism is discernible in the impoverishment and trivialization of the doctrinal content of religious belief. This latter is eloquently described by Hugh O'Donnell's lines concerning a

5.   Harvey Cox, *Seduction of the Spirit*, (London: Wildwood House), 1974, p. 221.
6.   John Hewitt, "Neither an Elegy nor a Manifesto", *The Selected John Hewitt*, p. 44.

teacher's treatment of the mystery of God's creative-redemptive activity:

Attention!
Today, we will finish creation.[7]

In confronting the effect that functionalism is having on Religious Education, we must avoid the twin dangers of a pessimism that leads to a nervous withdrawal from reality and an optimism that ignores reality. What is necessary is an approach which initiates the recovery of those elements that are in danger of being lost.

One of our primary focuses for the future must be on one particular element that underlies the whole enterprise of Religious Education, that is, the recovery of the symbolic imagination. The symbolic is the point of integration of life, experience, religion and as such it is intrinsic to the aims and objectives of Religious Education.

By the symbolic here is understood an approach to understanding and interpreting reality which is distinct from the scientific and the properly functional. The former analyzes in order to distinguish and understand objectively. The latter quite rightly describes reality in terms of its uses and functions. The symbolic gathers up the functional and the scientific and moves us into reality at the level of self-conscious involvement which recognizes the depth-dimension of our experience of reality.

I take a risk in using the word symbolic. In our day there is an impoverishment of the notion. It is frequently interpreted as less than real, as operating exclusively at the affective level or as opposed to the conceptual and rational. The symbolic has suffered from all of these misinterpretations but when understood in its proper context it refers to an approach to reality which demands our existential involvement and which yields an understanding and interpretation of reality that is at once expressive and constitutive, affective and conceptual, experiential and reflective.[8]

Unless we can move within functionalism, recognize it for what it is, convert people to the recovery of the symbolic approach to religion,

7. Hugh O'Donnell, "Deschooling", in *Mrs Moody's Blues See Red*, (Limerick: Salesian Press), 1980, p. 10.
8. The following is a selection of sources from which a comprehensive understanding of symbol emerges: Karl Rahner, "The Theology of Symbol", *Theological Investigations*, vol. 4 (London: Darton, Longman & Todd), 1966, pp. 221-252; Eric Voeglin, "Immortality Experience, and Symbol", *Harvard Theological Review* 60 (July 1967) :235-279; Paul Ricoeur, *Freud and Philosophy* (New Haven: Yale University Press, 1970); Gregory Baum, *Religion and Alienation*, (New York: Paulist), 1975.

and engage in it ourselves, Religious Education will continue its tortuous twisting in the name of relevance and experience. This recovery has to take place at two levels. The first is the level of the experience of God, the second is the level of the meaning of that experience as expressed in the content of religion.

We begin with the experience of God.

He reveals himself to us in the depth-dimension of our ordinary human experience. If, however, our contact with that experience is superficial, unreflected, functional, then we cloud the vision of reality that penetrates the surface to the depth; the vision of which Brendan Kennelly speaks when he says. "But vision is not simply seeing straight."[9] Essential to this vision, this reflective approach to experience and reality, is an attitude of wonder and receptivity: an attitude that explores experience without destroying it; that interprets it without exhausting it; that tries to understand it without distorting it; that respects the Mystery that is at its heart. It is, on our part, an attitude in which our blindness is acknowledged, our frailty is felt. It requires of Religious Education a passionate commitment to wonder and question; to tiptoe rather than march through reality; to whisper rather than shout; to lisp rather than to claim exhaustive description. It is to recognize that we touch life most sacredly in this symbolic approach.

At the heart of this understanding of the symbolic approach to reality is the christian sacramental vision that sees the action of God, not as something that inserts itself from outside in an alien manner, but as something with which the world is penetrated and transformed. This is the theological foundation for a future focus. God is experienced by us in our unlimited reaching out towards freedom and love, in self-transcendence, in the depth dimension of our ordinary human experience.[10]

In a world that is exalting the functional, Religious Education must take a firm stand with all that encourages the experience of the depth-dimension of life: with wonder, reflection, the natural drive to self-transcendence which pushes us to the barrier of the question that questions questioning itself: the question that contains the question of God.[11] Religious Education must work to ensure that

9. Brendan Kennelly, "The Blind Man", *Selected Poems* (Dublin: Allen Figgis Ltd.), 1969, p. 17.
10. See Karl Rahner, *Foundations of Christian Faith* (New York: Seabury), 1978, pp. 42-54; *Spirit in the World* (London: Sheed & Ward), 1967, pp. 179, 180.
11. Bernard Lonergan, *Method in Theology* (London: Darton, Longman & Todd), 1971, pp. 102, 103.

functionalism does not suppress this experience of transcendence and, furthermore, its approach must recognize the fact that God reveals himself in the reality of experience in our day and not in some imagined reality where all is lightness and goodness.

Reality as we experience it today is not all positive. While it is true that beautiful sunsets and peace-filled prayer are part of our experience of God, they are not the norm. Aware of this, Religious Education must set about the recovery of the symbolic in a manner that perceives the darkness of our world and with a conviction that darkness is a special form of light in which God is as surely revealing himself as in the sunrise.

The recovery of the symbolic is also necessary at the level of meaning.

God's revelation of himself to us is in harmony with our experience of ourselves as self-transcending beings. In the dynamism of our existence there is to be found a gifted experience of Mystery. This experience of the Mystery of God's presence finds its ultimate expression in the life, death and resurrection of Jesus Christ.

The thematization and interpretation of God's revelation of himself is brought to a climax in Christ and is further expressed and interpreted in the doctrinal content of the christian church tradition. There is, therefore, an intrinsic continuity between God's revelation of himself, the fullness of that revelation in Christ and its continued reflective interpretation in the content of the faith as handed on by the Church.

This content is primarily expressed in the doctrines of the faith and these doctrines are the ". . . content of the Church's witness to Christ, they express the set of meanings and values that inform individual and collective christian living".[12]

In our day, functionalism affects our approach to the content of faith by asserting that it must submit rigorously to the logic of a functional analysis of truth. Thus the wrong criteria are applied and Religious Education falls into the trap of thinking that unless immediate usefulness and direct relevance to experience is perceived in the content of faith, there is no purpose in it or in teaching or preaching about it. Another, even more destructive approach prompted by functionalism, is to define and interpret the meanings of faith by paralleling them with factual human experience. The analogical and symbolic nature of language is thus denied and the content of faith is effectively evacuated of any meaning apart from that which can be practically experienced.

All of this results in an absence of doctrinal content in Religious Education or in an approach that allows for an arbitrary projection

12. Ibid., p. 311.

of meaning dictated by the demands of usefulness and a consequent impoverishment of the depth of meaning contained in the living tradition of the Church.

Hence, Religious Education must look closely at the way it is dealing with the content of religion, particularly its doctrinal content which is expressive and constitutive of the identity of both individual and community. The approach that has to be taken is the symbolic approach, in line with what has been said before in relation to the experience of God.

To speak of a symbolic approach here is neither reductionistic nor inappropriate. Rather it is to ensure that the content of religion truly serves to mediate identity, to move affectively, to urge to action, to offer understanding, to communicate beliefs. It is an approach that maintains the Mystery of revelation on the one hand, and its manifestation in experience on the other. It springs from the conviction that God's revelation of himself is in harmony with our experience of ourselves as human and it safeguards the fact that the meanings of religion have definitive cognitive content and a lasting claim to truth.[13]

If the content of religion gives expression to the meanings and values that inform individual and collective christian living, then they must function symbolically, that is, in a way that recognizes their inexhaustible depth as they speak of God's revelation in Christ in a manner that is self-involving.

The content of religion functions symbolically. That means that it presents the truth of God in Jesus Christ in a manner that is normative and constitutive and that ensures the inherent continuity between God's revelation of himself, that revelation as expressed in Christ, and its continued expression in the doctrinal tradition of the Church. The symbolic approach further safeguards the content of faith from an analysis that is overly or purely conceptual. It allows for the fact that the affective and experiential aspects of the content of religion are as intrinsic as the reflective and conceptual aspects. If doctrines are isolated from the experience that gave them birth, or from the reflective, conceptual analysis which delineates their meanings and interpretation, then they lose their power to mediate meaning and establish christian identity.

Thus it is that we can say that the meaning is there in the doctrines of the faith. It is guaranteed by the collective historical faith of the Catholic community and by the evidence of their christian praxis. It

13. See Avery Dulles, "The Symbolic Structure of Revelation", *Theological Studies* 41 (March 1980) : 51-73.

is likewise available in the tradition and teaching of the Church. But we must also hold that an attitude of receptivity and a willingness to take the time and trouble to grasp the meaning is the condition of its being authentically understood and experienced in faith. Hence, the meanings of the content of religion function symbolically, as bearers of meaning and truth and as mediators of christian identity, when they are appropriated through reflection and involvement. This appropriation demands commitment to the meaning of religion and its understanding. The believer must be involved. The Religious Educator must make a firm commitment to this involvement.[14]

This applies in both aspects that we have been considering: the experience of God and the content of that experience. The symbolic approach to both of these is a self-involving one and the self-involvement required is that of faith.

The criteria by which we can judge the authenticity of our self-involvement of faith are straight-forward. The authenticity of our christian values, relationships and actions is the judge of our claim to be involved and committed. Correlatively, the truth of revelation, rooted in experience and in Jesus Christ, is the source of such identity and praxis. The pseudo-character of a functional interpretation of the meanings of the content of religion will not survive the demands of praxis.

Finally, it must be said that a symbolic approach is above all an integrating one. It allows for the fact that the revelation of God in Jesus Christ evokes identity, interprets experience, integrates consciousness and calls to action. It counteracts a religious functionalism that sows seeds of religious apathy and indifference and it calls for commitment and involvement that is the praxis of a faith truly rooted in tradition.

So we come to future focus.

Religious Education has four primary objectives: to witness to Jesus Christ as the focal point of the whole historical process; to help people live in accordance with Kingdom values, critiquing all structures which contradict those values, which exploit the weak, deny human rights or downgrade the dignity of peoples; to witness to a hope that is rooted in the Paschal conviction that life will come out of death, good will triumph over evil, God's kingdom will come; to transform the society in which we live by the exercise of its prophetic mission that calls for decisions in the light of the Kingdom and measures all values and

14. See Rahner, "Theology of Symbol", pp. 224ff. Also Dulles, "Symbolic Structure of Revelation", pp. 67, 61; Ricoeur, *Freud and Philosophy*, pp. 17, 31.

judgments in faithfulness to the gospel. Underlying all this is Religious Education's task of initiating people into the Mystery of Christ and communicating the doctrines that interpret that Mystery.

Religious Education will continue to do the above effectively and in a lasting way only if it approaches the experience and content of religion in a non-functionalist manner. To do this a five-fold conversion is required:

1.   A conversion to reflection.

This implies a refusal to succumb to that contageous spirit of functionalism which trivializes our experience of reality and paralyzes our human urge to self-transcendence. It demands energy and commitment, that we live "at the hub and not at the rim of time".[15] Religious Education is not going to lead people to maturity of faith by encouraging a spectator attitude to religion. Religion does not present its meaning for inspection or its power for experience without the involvement of faith. Religious Education must therefore encourage an openness to experience, an enthusiasm for question and an energy that is both receptive and creative.

2.   A conversion to question.

The plea for security in our day brings with it a danger. It is the temptation to offer religion as the source of security for which the human spirit longs. Rather, religion raises the question of life, of meaning, of identity. Religious Education must help people feel safe and secure in the risk of question and to do that it must take the risk of faith.

3.   A conversion to language.

The language of religion is not simply informative. It is evocative, in the symbolic mode. The truth of religion is elusive and complex and cannot be expressed in technical equations. Its meanings, expressed in doctrines, must be communicated and interpreted to the believer. To refuse to give faith its expression in doctrine or to provide interpretation that challenges and constitutes identity, is to evacuate faith of its expressive and constitutive power. The content of faith must be integrative in the symbolic sense and to be such it demands energy and commitment to a symbolic approach to reality.

4.   A conversion to the pilgrim status of Religious Education.

Religious Education will never develop a prototype, a recipe, a formula that will eliminate the continual quest for new ways of incarnating the revelation of God and of humanity. So religious educators must strive for a sense of their own identity that will allow them to feel

15.   Richard Murphy, "Tony White", *The Price of Stone*, (London: Faber and Faber), 1985, p. 30.

safe with questions, secure in uncertainty and calm in the face of indifference. They must be able to accept their own incompleteness. Otherwise they will never accept the incompleteness of those to whom they minister.

5. Conversion to hope.

We have an option. We can be content to moan about the present, regret the past and fear the future. But if we choose to be Religious Educators then we must challenge, critique and redeem any form of complacency, passivity or ideology and one of the primary ways we do this is by being hopeful, and by offering hope that is grounded realistically in the saving, living word of God.

We have a tendency to become fascinated with the problems in a way that Yeats expressed well in the following:

> The fascination of what's difficult
> Has dried the sap out of my veins, and rent
> Spontaneous joy and natural content
> Out of my heart.[16]

So we can buy into the prevailing mentality and mourn the world. We can even provide suitable hymns and prayers for the wake! But at the heart of the christian message is a gospel vision and a faithful promise.

The vision is that of Christ's triumph over death and evil. The promise is that his continued presence empowers us and brings us the assurance of success, even in the midst of apparent failure. And that must be the conviction out of which we operate.

The word catechesis means to echo, to resound. But if there is no depth there is no echo and the depth of our echo depends on the quality of our immersion in the Mystery of which we speak. This is not just a pious hope. Our task is to proclaim Christ in a way that is alive and meaningful and full of vibrant life, which is tentative yet convinced, creative yet solidly rooted in his revelation and in the Church's tradition.

16. W. B. Yeats, "The Fascination of What's Difficult", *The Faber Book of Irish Verse*, (London: Faber and Faber), ed., John Montague, 1974, p. 232.

The Language of Catechesis

Donal Murray

For a description of the situation of catechesis today, and for an outline of the task that it faces, one need go no further than the opening paragraphs of the *General Catechetical Directory*:

> In times past, the cultural tradition favoured the transmission of the Faith to a greater extent than it does today; in our times, however, the cultural tradition has undergone considerable change, with the result that less and less can one depend on continued transmission by means of it. Because of this, some renewal in evangelization is needed for transmitting the same Faith to new generations. It should be noted that the Christian faith requires explanations and new forms or expression so that it may take root in successive cultures (GCD 2).

This cultural change particularly affects us in Ireland; we see a certain falling off in the rate of religious practice, the social acceptability of loose or non-existent Church allegiance and the public debate on moral issues, but there is more to it than that. These phenomena have been, after all, common in many countries for a long time. All over the world the cultural tradition has become less dependable as an aid to the transmission of the Faith because it has become *secularised*. That word does not explain what has happened nor why it happened; it does not describe the change very precisely, yet we all know what it means. Religion which in the past was seen as relevant to every moment and every sphere of life tends to become a compartment with its own limited place in the order of things, while the other compartments go about their business independently.

Church documents and preaching testify to this by constantly speaking of the need to break down the barriers between religion and life. *The Work of Justice*, for example, says, "one of the urgent needs in the Church today is to remove the partitions separating religion from life and tending to keep religion confined to Sundays and to churches"(WJ 5).

It is clear that this partition must have an impact on catechesis. Anyone who has taught a religion class will know that you can have a most lively and constructive lesson on the Third World, or discussing a film or story, or analysing the needs of the local community, or evaluating the media but there comes the awful moment when the teacher says, "Does that remind you of anything in St. Matthew's Gospel"? The question has an impact rather like a commercial break in the middle of an exciting film on television! The teacher has switched suddenly from a compartment of life which is stimulating and exciting to one which, though very important, is seen as dull. The class feels cheated. The catechist feels cheated too because he or she is dedicated to demonstrating that such partitions ought not to be unbridgeable, that religion is absorbing and exciting, that the gospel does shed light on the topic and allow it to be understood more deeply.

In that critical moment of attempted bridging of the gap between religion and life we see the challenge to catechesis today. There seems to be no easy link between the cultural tradition, between what one might simply call life in general, and the tradition of faith. The gap is the fundamental crisis that faces the process of catechesis.

The notion that faith is a separate compartment is one in which we cannot acquiesce. It may well be true that the culture in which we live contains, to a greater extent than in the past, elements which are foreign, or even hostile, to christian faith. This *cannot* mean that catechesis should be independent of its environment. If catechesis fails to address our culture in order that faith may take root in it, then it quite simply fails in its task.

To accept the gap between religion and life as an unchangeable truth would be to accept that religion is simply a compartment. That in turn would be to accept that God matters only in particular spheres of life. This would be self-contadictory. A god who is not always present, always sustaining creation, always calling us, would not be the God of the Bible. Unless God is recognized as Lord of the whole of life he is not recognized *as God*. The gap between religion and life is, therefore, potentially destructive of faith and of catechesis.

The first thing that must be done in analysing the task of catechetics today is to try to understand the causes of this gap which ought not to exist.

1. The Second Vatican Council spoke of "a real social and cultural transformation whose repercussions are felt too on the religious level" (GS 4). That transformation has many facets and it would be impossible to list them all. They would include:

(a) *The media explosion* which has meant that relatively isolated and unchanging communities have quite suddenly been exposed to outside influences. Many hitherto unquestioned principles and values and beliefs are seen, on a world scale, to be very much a "minority viewpoint". The burden of proof has dramatically shifted. Ideas which a generation ago would have been dismissed as outrageous now tend to be seen as new, exciting and enlightened. This is particularly disorienting when, as we said, catechesis in the past was heavily dependent on the cultural support of accepted principles, values, and beliefs.

Even more fundamentally, perhaps, the new media have brought about new perceptions, new ways of seeing things in which the written word plays a smaller part than previously. As a group of delegates to the International Catechetical Congress in Rome in 1971 put it: "until recently, education spoke of 'audio-visual aids'. Today we are discovering a greater task. It is not a question of using audio-visual aids to present the message more effectively but rather of translating the Christian Message of Liberation — the Good News of the Gospel into the audio-visual language of people today." The transmission of faith in the past depended on the written and spoken word; other non-verbal ways of communicating ideas are active to a much greater extent today. If we fail, the expression of faith will be confined to particular aspects of the whole process of social communication.

(b) *The growth of urbanization* with the breakup of communities and a more anonymous, less supportive, lifestyle. A rural lifestyle, though it too had its own shortcomings, did involve a sense of belonging and an interaction with ones neighbours and of shared concerns that do not exist in the same way in a city. Life has become more compartmentalised — a person's work may be miles from home; one's real neighbours and one's recreation may be miles away in another direction. Life is no longer a unity but a collection of almost unrelated spheres. Religion is in danger of becoming just another compartment, or of being squeezed out altogether. Personal conviction and choice are now vital in a way that was not the case in a more cohesive Christian community.

(c) *The emergence of a whole new series of issues* such as concern about the just and urgent claims on us of developing countries, the role of women, nuclear weapons, the environment, to which the traditional presentation of faith does not provide ready-made answers. This can lead to the idea that the real questions and answers are to be found not in the tradition of faith but in the peace movements, the environmental movements, the feminist movement, the development organisations.

One could go on listing such factors indefinitely. I will simply point out, for the moment, that these are not unrelievedly negative things. Undoubtedly there are irresponsible uses of media; there is dehumanization in exessive and badly planned urbanization; there are exaggerations in any movement that devotes itself single-mindedly to pursuing an issue, however noble. On the other hand, a world of instant communication between peoples, with its new possibilities for mutual understanding, a world where personal conviction and commitment are called for if people are not to drift purposelessly, a world where moral issues are constantly debated and publicly pursued, must offer opportunities to catechesis which would not be present in other circumstances.

The conclusion for catechetics is that this social and cultural transformation means that it can no longer be assumed that the language in which the faith was handed down to recent generations is necessarily the language that speaks most effectively to people today. By language, I mean not just written or spoken words but the whole process by which we communicate with each other, words, symbols, hidden agendas and assumptions.

2. The second cause of the gap between religion and life is more internal to the life of the Church. This also raises problems of language.

(a) We should not underestimate the degree to which the Second Vatican Council, and the surrounding reflection and renewal, enriched our understanding of Christian faith. New ideas on the role of the Church in the world, on the liturgy, on revelation, on religious freedom, on ecumenism, on all sorts of areas, were percolating through the Church. This has resulted in often unspoken uneasiness about traditional symbols and ceremonies — Benediction of the Blessed Sacrament, religious art, sacramentals, familiar prayers; and about traditional language — 'sanctifying grace', 'the holy Sacrifice of the Mass', 'temperance', 'sin', 'chastity', even the word 'Catholic'. There is a whole list of words which are heard much less frequently than before.

This is not, in general, because of a rejection of the truths which these symbols or words express, but rather because of a fear that with all the overtones they had in the past, they may not convey, and may even obscure the full richness that we wish to communicate. This involves three dangers:

1. It is possible that what is out of sight is out of mind, that by failing to use the traditional words we may fail to communicate the truths that they express, leaving gaps because there are things for which the old word will not do and no new word has been found.

2. It is possible that these symbols, and more importantly these words may become the "possession" of people, and they

certainly exist, who have closed their minds to the renewal initiated by the Second Vatican Council.

3. It is possible that in neither using them nor replacing them with something that resonates as they did, we may leave ourselves without powerful words and symbols which appeal not only to the mind but to the heart and the memory.

The result of all this may be to leave theologians and catechists working with, or at least struggling towards, terminology and symbols — covenant, paschal mystery, eschatology, the sign of peace, icons, evening prayer — which are not new at all of course, but which lack the resonance of the older words and signs for people who have not grasped their significance and overtones.

(b) Even apart from the new theological insights, there has been in the last twenty years a growing realization of the need for what the *General Catechetical Directory* calls "some renewal in evangelization . . . for transmitting the same faith to new generations" (GCD 2). There is a realization of the new missionary challenge which faces us. Speaking of Europe, although the same thing might be said in slightly different ways for the rest of the world, Pope John Paul said recently: "the Europe to which we are sent out has undergone such cultural, political and economic transformations as to formulate the problem of evangelization in totally new terms. We could even say that Europe, as she has appeared following the complex events of the last century, has presented Christianity and the Church with the most radical challenge history has witnessed, but at the same time has opened the way today to new and creative possibilities for the proclamation and incarnation of the Gospel" (Pope John Paul II to sixth symposium of CEEC 11 October, 1985).

This freshness and creativity of the Gospel as it touches and transforms new situations involves a realization that many older ways of speaking and acting do not come to grips with the new lifestyle and the new challenges. There is a corresponding fear of jargon and cliché. If the Gospel is to become incarnate in a radically new situation then it clearly needs "new forms of expression" (GCD 2).

These theological factors, which are in many respects extremely positive, again point in the direction of seeking a new language for catechesis. On the other hand, and this is what makes the catechetical task today so difficult, it is not enough for the language of catechesis to resonate with the concerns and thought patterns of the present; it must transmit "the *same* faith to new generations" (GCD 2). There would be little point in catechesis being in touch with the world of the late twentieth century if it were out of touch with the tradition of faith. It cannot, therefore, be a case of "all changed, changed utterly, a terrible beauty is born"!

Most of the criticisms directed at modern catechetics concern this aspect, namely, whether it is sufficiently concerned to transmit the same faith. It is, perhaps, inevitable, but nonetheless worth noting, how rarely, by comparison catechists and text books are criticised for not being sufficiently in touch.

Some of those who accuse modern catechesis of not being true to the Church's tradition have clearly failed to grasp the significance of the sort of factors we have been considering. Some appear to believe that the Gospel could be effectively preached in the 1980's in the same way as it was in the 1880's. However blinkered and misguided it may be, such criticism can touch a raw nerve precisely because it expresses, even in caricature, a concern which no catechist can escape — the concern to be faithful to the unchanging faith in a changing world.

This is the tension which is expressed in the *General Catechetical Directory*: "By drawing the truth from the Word of God and faithfully adhering to the secure expression of this Word, catechesis strives to teach this Word of God with complete fidelity. . . The language will be different for different age levels, social conditions, human cultures and forms of civil life" (GCD 34).

"The language will be different", but if the underlying message is not the same Word of God, then catechesis has failed in the most radical way. The tension which is implied here cannot be resolved by appealing to some pure expression of the Word of God which stands above and apart from its cultural environment and which could simply be translated into our terms. The Gospel is always incarnate, as was the Word himself: "the words of God, expressed in human words, are in every way like human language, just as the Word of the eternal Father, when he took on himself the flesh of human weakness, became like human beings" (DV 13).

What is at stake, therefore, is not that each generation looks back to a disembodied Word which is then brought to bear on its own situation, but rather that each generation stands in continuity, first of all with its own immediate predecessors and then with all the generations stretching back to *the* Incarnation of God's Word in Jesus Christ: "On the one hand, the Gospel message cannot be purely and simply isolated from the culture in which it was first inserted... nor without serious loss, from the cultures in which it has already been expressed down the centuries; it does not spring spontaneously from any cultural soil; it has always been transmitted by means of an apostolic dialogue which inevitably becomes part of a certain dialogue of cultures" (CT 69).

Part of that process of transmission must clearly be a concern by any given generation that what it is transmitting is the gospel. Each generation wants to know that it can say with St. Paul: "I delivered to you as of first importance what I also received, that Christ died for our sins in accordance with the Scriptures, that he was buried and that he was raised on the third day in accordance with the Scriptures" (*1 Cor 15:3*).

So far, we have seen that catechesis today, perhaps more than at any time, has to face the challenge of finding new expressions of the same faith. We must turn now to the question of the characteristics which the new language of catechesis needs to have if it is to be true to the meaning of catechesis.

(1) *The language of catechesis must be complete*. The possibility of incompleteness arises in a number of ways. Faced with a whole series of new questions and priorities it is necessary to resist the temptation to present only those elements of the Gospel that seem particularly topical or appealing or useful. Catechesis is at the service of the Gospel and of the Church's tradition, not the other way around. "There would be no catechesis if it were the Gospel which had to change when it came into contact with the cultures" (CT 53). However new the language, it has to express the same Gospel.

It would be possible for an individual preacher or catechist to distort the message by filtering out everything that seemed awkward or strange — as many a "Thomist" did with the thought of Aquinas. In the same way, it would be possible for a particular generation to impoverish the message by omitting whatever seems not to be immediately intelligible or useful. This would be to present a god made in the image of, and responding to the needs and aspirations of, the Western European of the late twentieth century. Our question, our experience, our insights do not exhaust the Gospel. It is especially important in a time of such rapid change that we do not tie our presentation so closely to the 1980's that it will seem outdated and irrelevant in the 1990's.

That is the importance of Part Three of the *General Catechetical Directory* and of such documents as Pope Paul VI'S *Credo of the People of God*. If we were to present only those elements of the Gospel which seemed to meet our concerns we might fail to present those aspects which might speak most eloquently to the, as yet unknown, concerns of the twenty first century. We would be presenting a god of the 1980's rather than the God of Abraham, Isaac and Jacob and Paul and Augustine and Patrick and Brigid and Thomas Aquinas and Catherine of Siena and Maximilian Kolbe.

Incompleteness might arise in another way too. It might arise from "playing safe", from sticking to ground that seems firm underfoot. In the area of morality, for example, the tradition is quite clear about certain questions of sexuality, of justice, of the right to life and so on. It is right that these should be presented with the clarity that they have, with the reasons which lead to that clarity and expressed in a language that carries conviction to people today. But it is also true that there are other questions, for the most part questions that have not been posed in the same way to previous generations, questions about new possibilities in the field of medicine, of weaponry, of technology, where our answers are less clear. This is partly because of the complexity of these questions and partly because we do not have the benefit of seeing how previous generations of Christians evaluated them.

Clarity is not, however, the same as *importance*. The fact that the Church's position on some of these issues is not, or is not yet, as clear cut as on other matters, does *not* mean that they can be ignored or that they should be regarded as unimportant. The fact that we cannot say in detail how the resources of the state should be applied, or how nuclear disarmament should be achieved, or how to achieve the balance between environmental interest on the one hand and useful but polluting industries on the other, would not justify us in giving the impression that such questions were outside our concern as Christians: "The joy and hope, the grief and anguish of the people of our time, especially of those who are poor or afflicted in any way are the joy and hope, the grief and anguish of the followers of Christ as well. Nothing that is genuinely human fails to find an echo in their hearts" (GS 1).

Catechesis deals in certainties, but it must also direct the light of the Gospel to that task of conscience in which, "Christians are joined to the rest of humanity in the search for truth and for the right solution to so many moral problems which arise both in the life of individuals and from social relationships" (GS 16). To fail to do so would be simply another form of confining the Gospel to areas in which we felt it would be at home, domesticating and limiting the Gospel.

Incompleteness could arise, finally, from a lack of balance: "Integrity does not dispense from balance and from the organic hierarchical character through which the truths to be taught, the norms to be transmitted, and the ways of Christian life to be indicated will be given the proper importance due to each" (CT 31).

The desire to present the whole tradition could result in losing sight of the wood for the trees. The old catechism said that "the principal mysteries of religion are the Unity and Trinity of God, the Incarnation,

Death and Resurrection of our Saviour". The "organic hierarchical character" of catechesis would demand that these truths would be seen as central and other truths seen in their relationship to that core.

In practice, however, this hierarchy of truths was often far from clear. It was just as important for children to be able to recite the answer to the question, "Is it lawful to take part in games and other amusements on Sundays?" as the question, "Did Christ rise from the dead?" This lack of awareness of the order or pattern of truth was reflected in what was quite a common trick question when I was growing up: "What is the most important feast of the year?" The vast majority of people, what we might be tempted today to call the "sensus fidelium", would reply "Christmas". The primacy of Easter was not a very intelligible curiosity. This was hardly surprising when one thinks that in the 1951 catechism there are only three questions on the Resurrection: "Did Christ rise from the dead?" "What does the Resurrection of Christ prove?" "How long did Christ remain on earth after his Resurrection?"

The language of catechesis must be complete in the sense that it expresses not just a list of truths, all of which are equally true; it must also express the fact that these truths are not equally central, that they form an organic whole: "On all levels, catechesis should take account of this hierarchy of the truths of Faith" (GCD 43).

This is not an easy demand. It was not, as I have suggested, particularly well achieved in the recent past. It will always be rendered more difficult because one must take account not just of the relationship by which some truths depend upon and illuminate other more important truths, but also of the fact that at any given time particular truths, not necessarily the most important in themselves, may be challenged, or in danger of distortion, or likely to be ignored. Such truths may, therefore, require special attention, but this must be done without exaggerating their importance in a way which would obscure "the hierarchy of the truths of Faith".

This balance is the result of constant effort. The central core of Faith remains unchanged in the "principal mysteries of religion", but keeping that focus right is what Chesterton called the Church's "great and daring experiment of the irregular equilibrium": "People have fallen into a foolish habit of speaking of orthodoxy as something heavy, humdrum and safe. There never was anything so perilous or so exciting as orthodoxy... To have fallen into any one of the fads from Gnosticism to Christian Science would indeed have been obvious and tame. But to have avoided them all has been one whirling adventure; and in my vision the heavenly chariot flees thundering through the ages, the dull heresies sprawling and prostrate, the wild truth reeling but erect",

(G.K. Chesterton, *Orthodoxy*, Sheed & Ward, London 1939, pages 167-9).

That balance can be achieved only by returning constantly to the core of God's revelation in Christ, in order to be able to give to what Pope John Paul called "the bewildered and restless world of today" the gift of christians "who are confirmed in what is essential and who are humbly joyful in their faith" (CT 61).

(2) *The language of catechesis must be a shared language*. However much we need to find "new forms of expression", it is also necessary to ensure that the expression of faith is recognizably continuous with that of previous generations. Catechesis involves memory. As the Message of the 1977 Synod of Bishops put it: "This is another primary aspect to the action of the Church: to recall, commemorate, and celebrate acts of worship in memory of the Lord Jesus... Thus to be a christian means to enter into a living tradition, a tradition which, through the history of human kind, reveals how in Jesus Christ the word of God took on human nature" (Message 9).

That living tradition has its own language and it does not seem possible to communicate that tradition without what *Catechesi Tradendae*, quoting Archbishop Dermot Ryan, called, "a certain memorization of the words of Jesus, of important Bible passages, of the Ten Commandments, of the formulas of Profession of the Faith, of the liturgical texts, of the essential prayers, of key doctrinal ideas ...' (CT 55).

Without familiarity with the Beatitudes and the Lord's Prayer, without a Creed, without the liturgical responses, without words such as "Incarnation", "Trinity", "Redemption", "Salvation", "Sacrament" and "Eucharist", Faith would be in grave danger of being contentless or so vague as to evaporate. Christians would not have a common language in which to speak to one another or in which to worship together.

In this context, however, it is good to ask ourselves the question with which Pope John Paul introduced this point: ". . . Should we not attempt to put this faculty (of memory) back into use in an intelligent and even an original way in catechesis...? (CT 55).

The days are gone, and they are no loss, when a teacher waving a strap could terrify a class with the words, "for tomorrow, God help anyone who can't recite the Beatitudes down as far as "Blessed are the meriful".

A great deal of memorization can take place, almost spontaneously, through repeated use of prayers, through the use of musical settings — many people now know "The Lord is my Shepherd" who never

127

knew a psalm before. Others, thanks to Boney M, know, "By the Waters of Babylon". Memorization today requires, in a way in which it did not in the past, the association of texts and words with music and images and events. Perhaps indeed such a method might give a deeper meaning to the phrase "learning by heart". The use of original ways of enabling people to remember and to understand the chief formulas and expressions which are part of the living tradition should be an important part of modern catechesis. As a character in Brian Friel's *Translations* put it: "... it is not the literal past, the 'facts' of history, that shape us, but images of the past embodied in language."

There are, of course, particular difficulties about this today. Bible texts, for instance, are less likely to be remembered because they are encountered in different versions. While this variety can be a help towards understanding, it is an obstacle to remembering. The use of the Nicene Creed in the Mass has effectively blotted out the ability to recite either The Apostles' or the Nicene Creed for many people. It still remains a task for catechesis to bear in mind. As Father Denis Carroll pointed out in an article in *The Irish Catechist*, memory has a role to play both because religion has an "information content" and because memory can help understanding: "even yet we enrich our minds by good poetry. We still are glad to have the apt quotation to elicit understanding. Surely the same applies — analogously — to the cherished expressions of faith" (*The Irish Catechist* Volume 2 no. 2 page 12).

There is, however an even more serious difficulty. If we accept that "new forms of expression" are required, how can we ensure that these "new forms" are shared by the wider community? Catechetical renewal has taken place primarily and most effectively in schools. How far is the new language in which that has been expressed a language shared with parents, priests and the community in general? This has implications even for the question of memory. Something which is learned in school and never heard again at home or in daily life is most unlikely to be retained, especially in a world so full of information and stimuli as ours.

Even more importantly, if the language of catechesis is not shared by the whole community, if the "new forms of expression" communicated in school are greeted with incomprehension or suspicion, if they are treated as mere childish things about which adults need not concern themselves, the whole catechetical process is threatened: "Catechesis runs the risk of becoming barren if no community of Faith and Christian life takes the catechumen in at a certain stage of his or her catechesis. That is why the ecclesial community at all levels has a twofold responsibility with regard to catechesis: it has the responsibility of providing for the training of its members, but it also has the responsibility of welcoming them into an environment where thay can live as fully as possible what they have learnt" (CT 24).

The gaps which often exist between home and school, and between church and school, play into the hands of the tendency to compartmentalise. If there is one form of religious language for school and different forms for home or church, religion is, to that extent, not a unifying factor giving meaning to the whole of life but part of the divisions. If the language learnt in school is not echoed at home and in the parish then how is it to be a language that comes to grips with life?

Catechesis *needs* liturgy; it needs family life; it needs community involvement; it needs the dialogue of the generations; it needs to address itself to the groupings and relationships, to the emotions and commitments of the hearers, to speak to wherever people are and to everything they are; it needs to shed light on every aspect of life and culture. Catechesis is for the whole of life because God is the creator and redeemer of the whole of life. It would be quite simply impossible to catechize one aspect of life without reference to the rest.

One should not, perhaps, exaggerate this difficulty. It is not as if no renewal had taken place in the wider community; it is also true that the school itself can provide instances of liturgy, social involvement, the dialogue of the generations, and so on. Nonetheless, it has to be said that the call for home, parish and school to be involved together in catechesis rings uninterruptedly down the sixteen years since Fr. Pat Wallace and myself arrived in this Institute. Here, at least, is one element of the catechetical scene which seems immune to change!

In an ideal world, everything that needs to be done could be done at once. In reality, it would probably not have been possible to devote the necessary resources to developing adult religious education on a large scale while at the same time undertaking the renewal of school catechesis. It is, however, now time for us in Ireland to take very seriously the statement of the *General Catechetical Directory*: "Shepherds of souls should remember that catechesis for adults, since it deals with persons who are capable of an adherence that is fully responsible, must be considered the chief form of catechesis. All the other forms, which are indeed always necessary, are in some way oriented to it" (GCD 20, cf 96/97).

The catechetical renewal, ". . . a precious gift from the Holy Spirit to the Church of today. . ." (CT 3), had been a response to the challenge which Christianity faces today, "the most radical challenge history has witnessed" (Pope John Paul II). That response has, no doubt, like Chesterton's charioteer, reeled on occasion, but it is still erect! Any particular text book or programme, or indeed teacher, is imperfect. But criticism to be valid and worth taking seriously has to be made from within that attempt to respond to the radical challenge we face. "All Christians, according to the circumstances of their own lives and their special gifts or charisms are really involved in (catechesis). Indeed all Christians by virtue of Baptism and Confirmation, are called to transmit the Gospel and to be concerned about the faith of their brothers and sisters in Christ, especially of children and young people" (Message 12).

The language of catechesis must be a shared language because catechesis is the task of the whole Church and of every member. If the giving and receiving of catechesis is primarily carried on in one area of the Church, in schools and if "the principal form of catechesis" is not given the priority it deserves; if parents, priests and the whole Church are not sufficiently challenged to see catechetical renewal as *their* business, then we risk creating a tower of babel instead of a new Pentecost.

The language of catechesis must be a shared language in another sense too. It must be shared not just within the Church but with the wider culture. Clearly words like Trinity, Incarnation and Redemption are not going to be the common currency of a secular culture, nor will religious ceremonies be easily appreciated by it. At the same time, while giving answers enlightened by Faith, catechesis must show that it understands the questions of people today. It must speak in the audio-visual, multimedia language, which is not confined to the written word, it must show its awareness of the crises and anxieties, the hopes and possibilities that fill people's lives: "The human being, is the way for the Church, the way for her daily life and experience, for her mission and toil, the Church of today must be aware in an always new manner of the human 'situation'. That means that she must be aware of human possibilities... She must likewise be aware of the threats to humanity and of all that seems to oppose the endeavour 'to make human life ever more human' and make every element of this life correspond to true human dignity — in a word, she must be aware of *all that is opposed* to that process" (RH 14). Catechesis cannot be satisfied to speak a language that our culture does not know.

3. *The language of catechesis must call to conversion and give rise to hope.*
It would undoubtedly be possible to imagine a catechesis which would fulfill the other two criteria and yet fail to be true catechesis. *Catechesi Tradendae* rightly rejects the view that catechesis,

"necessarily rationalizes, dries up and eventually kills all that is living, spontaneous and vibrant in the kerygma". In order for that criticism to be untrue, however, it is necessary to have clearly in mind what the Pope goes on to say: "The truths studied in catechesis are the same truths that touched the person's heart when he or she heard them for the first time. Far from blunting or exhausting them, the fact of knowing them better should make them even more challenging and decisive for one's life" (CT 25).

This means, in the first place, that catechesis must touch the heart. In a phrase which Fr. Wallace drew to my attention in our early days here, "it is the change of heart that is the heart of the matter." The gospel is unchanging, but if those who hear it remain unchanged, then they have not understood it.

In the first place, this means that catechesis has to be concerned not only with being complete but with awakening conviction and personal conversion. In a more supportive culture, allegiance to the Church and the values of a christian way of life were almost part of the atmosphere people breathed. Today's catechesis must devote a far greater proportion of its efforts to strengthening of personal commitment. This is true even if that involves some diminution of the amount of detailed information than can be communicated in the time available. The response to this situation should not be an attempt to stuff in undigested information but to recognize that it is a further demonstration of the need for continuing religious education for adults. Information continues, of course, to be an important aspect of catechesis which should not be neglected even if other aspects now need greater emphasis than they did in the past.

Commitment cannot be taught from text books and syllabi; it can only be communicated by a person who already has it: "Catechesis demands the witness of faith, both from the catechists and from the ecclesial community, a witness that is joined to an authentic example of Christian life and to a readiness for sacrifice' (GCD 35). The maintaining and the strengthening of that commitment among catechists is both vital and difficult in the face of the tensions and difficulties which we have been considering. I suspect that we have not as yet, in Ireland fully appreciated the importance, and fully developed the potential, of an organization like the Catechetical Association of Ireland as a resource for the mutal strengthening of catechists in that commitment.

Catechesis has to present a moral ideal and specific conclusions from it which will reveal the shallowness and the selfishness and the dishonesty of our actions and attitudes. It has to awaken and intensify the "creative restlessness" in which "beats and pulsates what is most deeply human — the search for truth, the insatiable need for the good, hunger for freedom, nostalgia for the beautiful, the voice of conscience'' (RH 18).

This cannot be done simply as an academic exercise. These moral values have, of course, their application within the school and the school can provide some opportunity for pursuing them in the wider community. Nevertheless, one can see again how catechesis must limp if it is left to the school and how, ''an environment where they can live as fully as possible what they have learnt'' (CT 24) is essential to effective catechesis.

The language of catechesis has to challenge those who hear it — and that means that it must challenge those who speak it too — to see in their lives what could be but is not and what should not be but is. That is not achieved by rubbing people's noses in the dirt, by moaning about the state of the world; it is achieved by holding out the ideal of the Gospel values, seeing their truth and their power, and by recognizing the superficiality and absurdity of our lives without them.

It means recognizing that the obstruction of God's Rule in our attitudes and actions and omissions which we call sin is never a purely private matter. By sin, we diminish ourselves, we fail our community and our church, we reject and ignore the destiny which is our common purpose and which is God's gift.

That points to an even deeper touching of the heart that is required. The purpose of catechesis is to deepen the sense of God. Catechesis brings us face to face with the creative power which gave us and everything in the universe existence and which maintains all existence; it brings us face to face with the divine love which is stronger than sin or death or any evil; it brings us face to face with the mystery to which the only apt response is adoration. It brings us face to face with power and mystery and love in a sense that is infinitely greater than any experience we have of these realities in human affairs. Catechesis is inseparable from worship.

The reality of God revealed in Christ is not only a cause for adoration, it is a cause for thanksgiving. That mystery is revealed to us; that power saves us; that love is given to us. Precisely because we live in a less supportive, pluralist, culture, the Directory reminds those engaged in the ministry of the Word that they should, ''present the good news of Christ in its remarkable character both as the mysterious key to understanding the whole human condition and as a free gift of God which is to be received by means of heavenly grace upon admission of one's own insufficienty'' (GCD 3).

The transformation of the individual in terms of commitment, morality and worship is possible through the proclamation of the Good News that God loved us first. In order to convey that possibiltiy, the language of catechesis must be a language of hope. It brings the memory of Christ's revelation to bear on the reality of today in order to reveal the destiny of that reality. "Embracing with a lively sense of history the rich and multiform patrimony of ideas of the past, we must open up to the present with a spirit of trust and project ourselves in hope towards the future. Prophecy must spring from memory" (Pope John Paul II, Symposium of CEEC 11 October, 1985).

The purpose of education, and even more fundamentally of religious education, is not to prepare unquestioning and compliant cogs for the smooth running of society as it is. It is to prepare people to be constructively critical, to take responsibility, to recognize the need for change. It is to give people a vision of human dignity and human purpose against which the shortcomings of any society can be judged and in the light of which something more human can be pursued. One need only take a sentence from each of Pope John Paul's encyclicals to crystallise this point:

> There is already a real perceptible danger that, while human dominion over the world of things is making enormous advances, humankind should lose the essential threads of its dominion and in various ways let humanity be subjected to the world and become something subject to manipulation in many ways — even if the manipulation is often not perceptible directly — through the whole of the organization of community life, through the production system and through pressure from the means of social communication (RH 16).

> A world from which forgiveness was eliminated would be nothing but a world of cold and unfeeling justice, in the name of which each person would claim his or own rights vis-à-vis others; the various kinds of selfishness latent in people would transform life and human society into a system of oppression of the weak by the strong, or into an arena of permanent strife between one group and another (DM 14).

> ...The error of early capitalism can be repeated whenever a person is in a way treated on the same level as the whole complex of the material means of production, as an instrument and not in accordance with the true dignity of his or her work — that is to say when he or she is not treated as a subject and maker, and for this very reason as the true purpose of the whole process of production (LE 7).

The catechist is saying in fact, as Tennyson put it: "Come my friends, 'tis not too late to seek a newer world."

Catechesis plays its role in the task of what the Pope has called "giving a soul to modern society" (CEEC Symposium). It does so by showing that not only are human and religious values of which it speaks the really important things but also by showing that they are eternal. The Gospel presents a set of values which overturn the calculations of possessions and power and prestige. The widow did not just "do her best, God love her", she put in "more than all of them" (Luke 21:3); "Who ever would be first among you must be your slave" (Mt 20:21); "Truly I say to you they have received their reward" (Mt 6:16).

The things that really count are eternal: "After we have spread on earth the fruits of our nature and enterprize — human dignity, brotherly communion and freedom — according to the command of the Lord and in his spirit, we will find them once again, cleansed this time from the stain of sin, illuminated and transfigured..." (GS 39).

That is why the language of catechesis should not be dull and deadening; these are the words of eternal life. They present Jesus Christ who is, "the goal of human history, the focal point of the desires of history and civilization, the centre of humankind, the joy of all hearts and the fulfillment of all aspirations" (GS 45).

Abbreviations

DM	*Dives in Misenicordia*
DV	*Dei Verbum*
GS	*Gaudium et Spes*
LE	*Laborem Exercens*
RH	*Redemptor Hominis*

Education as Liberation

Kevin Nichols

In recent years, 'Liberation' had become a powerful and seminal word in many different areas of life and thought. Even the Sacred Congregation for the Doctrine of the Faith — no great lover of the word and what it stands for — has acknowledged this. "The powerful and almost irresistible aspiration that people have for liberation constitutes one of the principal signs of the times which the Church has to examine and interpret in the light of the gospel" says its *Instruction*. It adds "the desire for liberation finds a strong and fraternal echo in the heart and spirit of Christians."[1] This interpretation of the signs of the times cannot be restricted to reflection on disembodied aspirations. It must also consider how these are cashed out in human institutions and movements. Among these, education is prominent. It continues to be a powerful force in the world; even if it is often made a dumping-ground for intractable problems beyond the capacity of its institutions. The main purpose of this lecture is to examine educational thought and practice in the light of the theme of liberation.

To couple the words 'education' and 'liberation' is to evoke almost inevitably the name of Paolo Freire. Indeed I shall be considering his thought, especially as it is expressed in *Pedagogy of the Oppressed*[2] a classic which no-one concerned with education in the world can ignore. Still, let us begin nearer home. David Jenkins, the Bishop of Durham has recently urged that we, in the West, should work to produce a Liberation Theology of our own,[3] in our own countries. "The question is not 'how can we adapt theology to our own needs?' but rather 'how can our needs create a theology which is our own?'" ' The tradition of Western education has a Janus-like character, looking

1. Sacred Congregation for the Doctrine of the Faith: *Instruction on certain aspects of Liberation Theology* C.T.S. London, 1984 pp 5 and 7.
2. Freire, P., *Pedagogy of the Oppressed*, Penguin 1972.
3. Jenkins D. E., *The God of Freedom and the Freedom of God*, Hibbert Trust, 1985, p 9.

towards the past and the future, towards the individual and society, towards conformity and questioning. Many years ago, Percy Nunn spoke of its conservative and creative purposes.[4] Frederick Clarke wrote that its business is "to communicate the type and provide for growth beyond the type".[5] More recently, philosophers such as R. S. Peters and Paul Hirst have argued that it is concerned both with initiation and also with rational reflection and autonomy.[6] We may trace this back to the way Plato coupled an insistence on eternal forms as the true objects of education with a Socratic method designed to promote critical thought.

This Greek ideal, rooted in the pursuit of reality or truth and in the fulfilment of the individual mind, bears the name liberal or free. This proud title has often been called a cruel parody. For it names the education given to a few free men whose lives were sustained by innumerable slaves. Not only were these slaves excluded from the literate world but whatever pertained to their work, their skills or abilities, their training, whatever could be labelled 'vocational' or 'useful', was dismissed as servile. Modern advocates of liberation would certainly condemn a system so aristocratic, so elitist. Liberation they would say, concerns the oppressed many, not the mental cultivation of the privileged few. Yet the tradition of liberal education survived the total collapse of the society it served. It survived the disappearance of the metaphysical doctrines on which it was based. Give or take a few sea-changes, it is alive and well today. Why is this?

The reason is that despite the blinkered narrowness of its concept of humanity, despite the politics of the stockade, the laager, the Pale, this tradition was, up to a point, the embodiment of a truly liberating force. First, it frees the mind for its proper function. It envisages and promotes pure rather than applied knowledge; so that life can be based on what is the case rather than on what men can, by trial and error achieve. It insists, with the Fathers of the Second Vatican Council that technical progress is not the greatest human priorities.[7] It opposes Bacon's "knowledge is power" because that represents the dominance of things and situations and is a prelude to that unexamined life which, according to Aristotle, is not liveable by men.

4. Nunn, P., *Education: Its data and First Principles*, Arnold, 3rd Edition, 1945.
5. Clarke, F., *Freedom in the Educative Society,* Routledge and Kegan Paul, 1949.
6. Cf. Peters, R.S. *Ethics and Education*, Allen and Unwin 1966, Chts. 1 and 2.
7. Flannery, A. (ed.) *Vatican Council II Documents*, p 934.

Secondly, an effective liberal education liberates its subjects from an unreflective acceptance of the world as it is, and establishes them as thoughtful critics of the status quo. We read in the psychologist Jean Piaget that the climax of the stage of formal reasoning is "the ability to conceive that the world could be run in a different way".[8] This truth that education can at least notionally subvert the established order was one of the hard lessons learned by the great imperial powers in their later years. They found that if you set up in colonies, centres of liberal education, they quickly become centres of disturbing nationalist and social aspirations. In our own time the Marxist powers are discovering the same hard truth. It is a lesson which should be deeply pondered also by the Catholic Church as its network of schools and colleges is drawn increasingly into the educational mainstream. Education is a risky business.

Thirdly, although liberal education may do no more than develop concepts and forms of logic which cause an itch of the mind, it may go beyond that. It may lead to self-possession, to that thoughtful and realistic self-acceptance which nowadays, is so necessary for the good life. It may even result in a reflective, a judged commitment to values. It may empower that "free adherence to God in faith" which the Church asserts to be the true goal of Catechesis.[9]

These aspects of Western education are all on the 'creative' side, favouring the person against social order, autonomy against transmission, the individual talent against tradition. They go far to explain why the long marriage between liberal education and Christian faith has had its bad patches, why indeed a strong strain of unease has run consistently below its surface. In the early centuries, some learned and holy fathers would have nothing whatever to do with Greek education for their flock. St Jerome's "Quid Athenae Hierosolymis" stands as the watchword of this view. These fathers stood against Greek learning not only because it was pagan in its content, but also because they feared its sceptical temperament. Not only might the morals of their neophytes be tainted but more seriously, their minds might be disturbed. We may feel we can discard St Jerome as a crusty old high Tory with Ciceronian indigestion. But the thought of John Henry Newman is much closer to the fibres of our minds. His, the most famous of all lectures on liberal education, were delivered just a short distance from here. In his earlier lectures, Newman elevates liberal education and its product the "philosophic habit" to great

8. Piaget, J., *The Psychology of Intelligence,* Routledge and Kegan Paul, London.
9. Cf. *The General Catechetical Directory*, C.T.S. London, 1972.

heights. "It is almost prophetic from its knowledge of history; it is almost heart-searching from its knowledge of human nature; it has almost supernatural charity from its freedom from bitterness and prejudice; it has almost the repose of faith because nothing can startle it."[10] Yet in mid-flight Newman seems to hesitate, check and change direction. Perhaps those liberally educated may become proudly self-sufficient and so undermine their faith. They may become "victims of an intense self-contemplation".[11] They may indeed. To this serious objection to the tradition of liberal education, I shall return in a few moments.

If St Jerome and Newman suspect liberal education for its sceptical, critical temperament, Paolo Freire's objection is of quite a different kind. He thinks it too conservative. It is the banking concept of education, an instrument of oppression used by the establishment to mould the young into its own world picture, to "annul the students' creative power and to stimulate their credulity".[12] Sufficient has been said about the virtues of the liberal tradition to show that this is a quite unfair generalisation about Western education. Rather than credulity, liberal education aims to promote rationality and personal autonomy. However, perhaps what Freire has in mind is what Paul Hirst has called the "forms of knowledge". In his able account,[13] Hirst argues that there are several distinct forms or ways of knowing, each with its own distinctive concepts, truth-tests and methodology. These are the empirical, the mathematical, the aesthetic etc. Perhaps Freire thinks that it is in organising knowledge in these ways, in giving prestige to certain modes of thought, that an oppressive establishment "stifles creativity" and domesticates the young.

Other writers have argued the case for organised knowledge as oppression, notably M.F.D. Young and his colleagues in *Knowledge and Control*.[14] In this book, a group of sociologists set out to "explore the implications of treating knowledge or 'what counts as knowledge' as socially constituted or constructed".[15] Their conclusions are similar to Freire's. The organisation of knowledge is not rooted in the nature of things. It is a device used by establishments to determine what shall count as success or failure and to ensure that

10. Newman, J.H., *On the Scope and nature of University Education*, Dent, 1939, p 131.
11. Newman, *op. cit.*, p 187.
12. Freire, *op. cit.*, p 49.
13. Hirst, Paul H., *Knowledge and the Curriculum*, Routledge and Kegan Paul, 1974, Chts, 4 and 6.
14. Young, M.F.D. (ed) *Knowledge and Control*, Collier Macmillan, 1971.
15. Young, *op. cit.*, p. 5.

success reflects their own world-view. All knowledge is shrouded in ideology. In revealing this, sociology exposes the establishment's hidden curriculum and liberates those oppressed by it.

It is not hard to see the holes in this case. Anthony Flew has expressed them forcefully.[16] If there is to be rational discussion, if there is to be coercive evidence, if true conclusions are ever to be reached, there must be necessary rules of logic, and knowledge must have some structure more solid than provisional earthworks thrown up by succeeding generations. Still, I am left with the feeling that this argument does not really answer Freire's attack on educational banking. His case is not only that in this system, knowledge is an unchanging and sterile stock, but also that some one has a heavy personal investment in it. The forms of knowledge do reflect a certain mind — a noble one as Newman said, but one among several. Paul Hirst in defending them acknowledges that they may change — slowly perhaps imperceptibly, but really.[17] Even the categorical concepts which constitute the form may alter. Through these chinks a whiff of relativism seeps in. The forms are thus. They could be otherwise. Perhaps the reasons why they are thus, are not what they seem. Perhaps liberal education has not survived the collapse of its metaphysical foundations as well as we thought. What it needs to hold firm is a unified theory of knowledge such as that put forward by Bernard Lonergan. He would not deny that knowledge often is organised and ranked by the power of social structure. But these cases he would say, are examples of group and general bias, examples of the difficulty we experience in keeping intelligence central to human life. We should look first not at the concepts and methods by which knowledge is at present organised into forms. We should look first at "the human mind that operates in all fields and in radically the same fashion in each".[18] This idea of the invariant structure of human knowledge in all fields including social action, value and faith, goes a long way to meet Freire's objections to the Western style of education. "Liberating education" he writes, "consists in acts of cognition, not transferrals of information."[19]

In the light of the three authors I have referred to, Newman, Lonergan and Freire, I go on now to consider a major weakness which appears in the tradition of liberal education when it is presented as liberation. This is the view that education should be neutral or value-

16. Flew, Anthony, *Sociology, Equality and Education,* Macmillan, 1976.
17. Hirst, P.H. *op. cit.,* p. 95.
18. Lonergan, B.J.F., *Insight,* Darton, Longman and Todd, 1958.
19. Freire, *op. cit.,* p 53.

free. It should not take sides in contentious questions. Ideas, principles and values should always be put forward along with the publicly accessible evidence which supports them and only with the force that evidence justifies. The concept of education — so it is argued — logically entails this because of its definitive criteria: an initiation into forms of knowledge set in a rational tradition which encouraged personal autonomy. In education we ought to help people to think for themselves, to assess evidence and to learn the skills involved in making decisions, forming commitments and loyalties. Education should distance itself — useful but detached, like a catalyst in a chemical reaction, like a midwife in a birth — from the vigorous, sprawling, logically untidy life of social movements, moral values and religious faith. To take the plunge into these waters is incompatible with the concept of education. It is often described by the less complimentary word, 'partisan'.[20]

To dig into this word a little is to uncover a weakness in this canon of public evidence, this division of knowledge into a hard realm of public certainties and a soft one of informed doubts. The dictionary definition of 'partisan' is "an adherent of a cause, especially an unreasoning one". Yet it also contains associations of military action. Partisans are guerrilla fighters; they fight against a powerful regime. Usually they are thought to be idealists. The cause they fight for may be irrational but there is implication that it is also just. So the word partisan is a double-edged sword. It is meant as a boo-word (unfair, special pleading, sectional interest). But half-way it turns into a hurrah-word and the partisans come to be seen as fighting to overcome a tyrannical regime of the mind. This regime is the canon of public evidence which forces knowledge (and so education) into a Procrustean bed from which it arises rickety and emaciated.

Why should we call the canon of public evidence tyrannical? In *The Grammar of Assent*, Newman argues against Locke's version of this canon, in terms of his "A priori evidential theory". Locke argues that "it is not only illogical but immoral to 'carry our assent above the evidence that a proposition is true', to have a surplussage of assurance beyond the degrees of that evidence".[21] Newman remarks of this that Locke "consults his own ideal of how the mind should act instead of interrogating human nature as an existing thing as it is found in the world".[22] His case is not that people are intellectually imperfect.

20. Wilson, J., *Education in Religion and the Emotions,* Rultledge and Keegan Paul.
21. Newman., J.H. *The Grammar of Assent*, Longman's 1889, p 163.
22. Newman, *op.,cit.*, p 164.

It is that "pure public evidence" is not something which really exists. Like the idea of "pure nature" it is a useful logical invention. The relation between assent and evidence is much less clean-cut. Assents exist without adequate warrants. They collapse while evidence remains. Prejudices can impede them. Forces intervene which are not pure evidence, yet which are not irrational either. They may be a cumulation of probabilities. Emotion may enter in, in a way which is not clouding but insightful. Moral factors — good will, a readiness to live with the consequences of our assents — may play a part. The 'evidential calculus' represents a thin and abstract notion of evidence. In the real world the structure of assent is many-sided. It represents a fuller idea of knowledge than the evidential calculus allows. Surely Lonergan is right in saying that "human knowing involves many distinct and irreducible activities: seeing, hearing, smelling, touching, tasting, inquiring, imagining, understanding, conceiving, reflecting, weighing the evidence, judging. No one of these activities, alone and by itself, may be named human knowing."[23]

Now in education, we want to deal with real assents. We want to help people to see, hear, inquire, understand, reflect, weigh evidence and also to act. We do not want people to be so attuned to the nuances of evidence and proof that they are perpetually revising their views, are totally lost in process, suffer from a paralysis of action. So if the evidences involved in a case are complex or go beyond public check and control, if they involve feelings, judgements and commitments, then ways must be found of deploying these in the educational process. Otherwise how will that process touch assents? How can it do other than remain at the level of concept and inference: an education for cleverness in judgement, skill in analysing political and social issues, subtle insights into religious experience? And in this case, will not the forces that really generate assent remain outside the educational pale in a jungle of tradition and prejudice?

It is time that if we introduce into education less precise and more personal kinds of evidence, it will be harder to respect the vulnerability of others. Adults as well as children are vulnerable in education and can be influenced in ways which are quite the reverse of liberation. I doubt if there are any techniques for guarding against this. The style of education I have in mind is well expressed by Martin Buber: "speech from certainty to certainty though from one open-hearted person to another".[24]

23. Lonergan, B.J.F., *Collection*, Darton Longman and Todd, 1967, p. 222.
24. Buber M., quoted in Hulines, E.D.A., *Commitment and Neutrality in Religious Education*, G. Chapman, 1979. p. 3.

The suggestion that it is the heart rather than the mind which should be open in education leads us from the logical question: what does education logically entail? To the moral one: how should educators act? In spite of theories about learning by doing it seems that our Western heritage of liberal education remains too cerebral, too abstract. "The native hue of resolution is sickled o'er by the pale cast of thought." To be liberated by it is only to be turned loose in the pastures of the mind. It is the education of the sophisticated, but uncontented mind. I introduce the word 'conversion' with some trepidation since it comes trailing clouds of raw emotion or evangelistic fervour. Bernard Lonergan takes it differently. There is a conversion of the mind, a moral conversion, a *Metanoia* which turns to God. Although they are outwardly dissimilar, they, like the act of human knowledge, have the same structure however realised. Error, misunderstanding, moral failure and the rejection of God spring from the same root. "The hopeless tangle of the social surd, of the importance of common sense, of the endlessly multiplied philosophies, is not merely a cul-de-sac for human progress, it is also the reign of sin, a despotism of darkness; and men are its slaves."[25] These powerful words do not recommend evangelical purgation. They assert rather that there is a movement of conversion in all true cognitional activity; intellectually from group and general bias towards attentiveness, reason and judgement; morally from egotism towards rational responsibility; religiously from partial insights to the primary intelligible, invulnerably known through the knowledge that arises from love. Thus, conversion from being anti-educational becomes a necessary educational goal at every level. Incidentally, through this understanding of conversion the gulf between overt religion and that which is implicit in human experience is bridged.

"Conversion to the people requires a profound rebirth. Those who undergo it must take on a new form of existence; they can no longer remain as they were."[26] Paolo Freire, for whom also, the idea of conversion is central. Taking sides, being neutral or partisan — these words for him do not speak of contentious propositions. They speak of solidarity with the oppressed of the world. Education is to liberate oppressed and oppressors alike.

Freire's book emerges from a very different conceptual world to that of Anglo-American philosophy. Man's task is humanisation, the greatest obstacle to it is the existence in the world of oppressors and oppressed. Educators must belong with the oppressed. They must

25. Lonergan, B.J.F., *Insight* P 692.
26. Friere, P.*op.cit.*, p 39.

142

eschew the banking concept in education whose curriculum represents the investment of the oppressors. Their method must be open-hearted dialogue about real-life themes which aim at action in the world and the dialectic of action-reflection-action which we call praxis. Reality is not established but is a process undergoing constant transformation. Educators must have a profound trust in man's creative power. Human life is an unfinished project which they must enable others to take into their own hands. So far as knowledge goes, what is wanted is cognition, not information; not the established *doxa* but the probing and creative *logos*. Education has a liberating function in that it forces people from oppression, and a revolutionary function in that it transforms the structures of the world.

Although their philosophical categories are so different, Freire's view and the Western liberal tradition do have one striking similarity. Both are concerned with standing on your own feet, with being critically conscious of the world, with taking your destiny in your own hands. In Freire's foreground stands reality as process and man as unfinished project. In Paul Hirst's view initiation into established forms of knowledge is highlighted. Both make emphatic use of words like 'critical' and 'autonomy' and so imply that they see education as a liberating force.

To balance what I have said about the weaknesses of the liberal tradition, I should like to make two criticisms of Freire's account of education. The first is that when compared with the cool logic of Western philosophy, his writing suffers from a certain cognitive confusion, even relativism. The key ideas like humanisation and oppression are never very closely examined. It is hard for us to grasp their logical geography. Again, the account of conscientisation of critical self-consciousness is rather diffuse. It is hard to be sure what this consciousness of self and of the world consists of: what key-concepts define it, what its methodology is, and what its tests for truth are. Lonergan's four watchwords for true human knowledge are: be attentive, be intelligent, be rational, be resspponsible. It is as though Freire took only the last of these seriously to heart, dissolving the others to lurk, anonymous presences in the ebb and flow of responsible action; as though this profound conversion of heart did not *necessarily* include conversion of mind.

Secondly, I have remarked that the theory of the 'forms of knowledge' has its limitations. These forms are not the eternal and necessary structures of thought. They have a slightly provisional air. They represent to some degree, the intellectual and social priorities of the leisured and prosperous West. Still, thought must have some structure, some worked out fields if anything is to be true. These are

143

established fields which we can find our way around. Among their strengths is the power of distancing; of seeing issues in the long perspective. In a broad context, in relation to other questions, of learning the lessons of history. In this way, the liberal tradition is the foil to another weakness which I believe we find in Freire's work. This I describe as the servitude of the immediate. It is a theory in which dawning self-consciousness is ringed by the circumambient present. It is therefore a consciousness which loses the heritage of the past, fails to grasp those insights which take centuries to gestate and be born.

The liberal 'critical openness' and Friere's 'critical self-consciousness' look-alike, blossom on the same hedgerow. How do they differ? First we notice the force of the word 'self'. This implies a large investment of personal capital, an active grasp not only of the inner self but also of the external circumstances which puzzle, influence or oppress. It is the committed consciousness of a person. 'Openness', on the other hand, suggests rather the cool detachment of a mind which welcomes events or ideas and inspects them with detached interest. It represents cognitive exactness against the warm human solidarity of dialogue. But the main difference between the two lies in the idea of action. Freire writes "thought has meaning only when generated by action upon the world." Only thought which is translated into and tested by action can play a part in that humanisation which is man's first task. I do not think that, as Christians, we need have any difficulty in accepting this Marxist idea that man exists to transform the world. It is indeed a truth of faith that man was made in God's image to be the steward, master and developer of God's creation. We should add that not all significant action is political, just as not all sin is social nor all oppression economic.

The Second Vatican Council teaches that "the achievements of the human race are a sign of God's greatness and the fulfilment of his mysterious design".[27] But there has existed among Christians, an ascetical attitude which regards the world as perishable, transient and worthless. In this view it is only the inner spiritual drama of contemplation and motive which counts. Only an 'ethical distillation', in Karl Rahner's phrase[28] is preserved, like flies in the amber of our inner selves. Our transforming work in the world crumbles into nothingness. Perhaps this outlook lingers subconsciously in the minds of some christians today. The teaching of the Council is that the inner renewal of grace is incarnated in our work in the world, The dimensions of interiority and bodyliness are not two parallel streams

27. Flannery, (ed) *Documents of Vatican II* p 934.
28. Rahner, K., *Theological Investigations*, Vol. 10. p. 270.

but two aspects of the integral person graced both in spirit and in world. So the liberation we are concerned with should envisage the integral person.

However, just as a little while ago, concern about interiority eclipsed the bodyliness of our faith, so quite possibly the opposite might happen. If we have been lost in wondering contemplation, we might shortly find ourselves lost in the tumult of action. That's the way the world wags. If a balance is to be held, we need to pay attention to both the elements. So, transforming action in the world crumbles into destruction and anarchy unless it is upheld by personal conversion of the heart. You can no more make a good world with bad people than you can make a good omelette with bad eggs. The two educational outlooks I have been discussing correspond to the two elements in this equation. At the heart of the liberal tradition lurks the thoughtful, well-informed individual, of developed sensitivity, adept at weighing evidence, attuned to the inner web of intention, motive and reason. Behind conscientisation stands a more robust figure, self-conscious as an active subject, squaring up to the social situations.

I come now to the last stage of my argument. You may have wondered what the practical application of my thesis might be. It is thus. In our Church we have never had a distinctive theory of education of our own. Usually we have adapted one from elsewhere; most often some version of the liberal tradition or an import from the field of catechesis. If we are to remain in education and make some distinctive impact then, I do not think this state of affairs can continue. In our time, the world of education is becoming much more self-aware and unified around a common concept of education, roughly a liberal-humanist one. This increasingly is accepted as embracing all aspects of education, including religion. Catholic schools and colleges are being drawn into the mainstream of this educational world, partly through economic necessity, partly through the greater solidarity in a common human effort which Vatican II said we should have. Now the danger in this development is that the distinctive character of Catholic educational institutions will dwindle like the Cheshire cat until nothing is left except a genial but meaningless smile. This would be, in my view, a disaster for the Church which ought to have a big stake in such a major human enterprise as education. It would also be bad for the educational world to be deprived of a challenging, if sometimes uncomfortable partner. It is not enough to say that we have a different ethos. That is not substantial enough, too ethereal, too difficult to cash out in hard facts. What is needed is a radical alternative view of education itself: not one which is unconnected with others but one whose unifying configuration is quite distinctive. I conclude by offering for discussion, five summary points which might form the groundwork of such a theory.

The first is to take seriously Freire's solidarity with the oppressed, that is, the evangelical option for the poor. These are to be found in increasing minorities in the developed West. Catholic education has often (by no means always) generously stood with the poor. A school inspector in the 1870's said that "only the Roman Catholic schools touch the very poorest". However, as society has become more fluid and more competitive, we have been drawn into the rat-race. We have been drawn into the general view that education should be a social ladder, an escape-hatch view for the able and deserving working-class child. This provision of a route whereby the oppressed may join the oppressors, is the reverse of Freire's view. We do not stand with the oppressed to make them bourgeois to provide, in the modish phrase, 'upward social mobility'. Catholic education should be distinguished by tirelessly looking for ways in which the disadvantaged can become aware of themselves, aware of their environment and able to transform it.

During the miners' strike in Britain last year it was observed that the miners' wives involved in the strike became politicised. Whatever one may think of the political stance they were drawn into, the process was instructive. Through action and reaction, success and failure, criticism and response, a new consciousness dawned; of themselves, their group, government and society: a new sense of strength, of having both the power and the responsibility to transform the world.

The second leitmotiv is the idea of conversion as an education goal. This includes the conversion of the mind from error, illusion, rationalisation, towards the truth: moral conversion from the pragmatic and the utilitarian towards commitment to values and responsible action; religious conversion to "the primary intelligible, known through the power of love". These are three embodiments of the same act of understanding in which the human knower turns towards truth and goodness. Conversion represents a christian penetration of the popular educational ideal of autonomy. Rather than acting as the whim takes us, or doing our own thing, it represents an act of self-possession which is also the possession of reality. In it the cognitive, the moral and the spiritual converge. True learning begins in wonder, goes on in humility and ends in gratitude.

Thirdly, a Christian idea of education will adopt the established forms of knowledge, respecting their structure, respecting rules of evidence, clarity, tests for truth. However, these forms of knowledge are not a priori categories, nor do they in themselves constitute the house of intellect built up on firm foundations. No, the forms of knowledge serve the greater task of humanisation, each according to its different mode of understanding. Each form is an instance of the act of human insight, diversely embodied but invariant in structure, no sharp line between commitment and neutrality, no 'no-go areas' in the curriculum.

Fourthly, and as Lonergan would say, penultimately, stands a deep faith in human creativity, as Freire puts it in "man's power to make and remake, to create and recreate".[29] This faith is based on the conviction that, despite our many failures, the Holy Spirit is at work in the transformation of the world. For Marxists that transformation has a specific terminus (and a rather thin one) in the dictatorship of proletariat or classless society. This marks the end of creativity (more a whimper than a bang) and the death of hope. For christians, God is our absolute future. So there is no specific limit to christian hope and no specific limit to human creativity. Joined to this faith and the hope it engenders must be a "profound love of the world and of men".[30] The mainspring of a christian idea will be that education is at its heart a work of love; and love of a particularly pure kind, which mirrors God's creative love in the growth of free persons who have charge of the world.

The fifth element is that christian education should always look towards action in the world as the pivot of its method. Once again, not all action is political. Some of you will be familiar with the See-Judge-Act method of Y.C.W., a profound educational idea which was somehow never capitalised. It was an early example of the rhythm of reflection-judgement-action-reflection-learning-further questions which now goes by the more fashionable name of praxis.

Finally, an idea of christian education would be realised in different concrete ways: as between one culture and another, between adults and children, between formal education and informal settings. Perhaps some of the points I have made will not hold up. I put them forward here, as Dr. Johnson said, "not dogmatically but deliberately". In any case, the building up of a coherent christian idea of education is a large task, far beyond one lecture or one book. This is as far as I can go:

> Keep Thou my feet I do not ask to see the distant scene, one step enough for me.

29. Freire, P., *op.cit.*, p 63.
30. Freire, p., *op.cit.*, p 62.

The challenge facing Religious Education today

Dermot A Lane

There are many challenges facing Religious Education today. To this
extent I must be selective in my approach to this broad and complex
subject. The area I wish to focus upon concerns the relationship
between Religious Education and the turn to social justice that has
become so prominent in the ministry of the Church in recent times.

Broadly speaking, my paper is made up of four parts. I will begin
by saying something about the general context in which Religious
Education finds itself today, with particular reference to the changes
and developments that have taken place over the last twenty years.
Then I will move on to give a preliminary description of the challenge
I see facing Religious Education today with a brief historical overview
of that challenge. Thirdly, I will analyse the details of this challege.
Fourthly, I will try to work out some of the practical implications
of the challenge.

Changes and developments affecting Religious Education
Historically speaking, I am conscious of the fact that in looking at
Religious Education just now we are doing so at a time when the
Church, both universal and local, has been looking back over the last
twenty years at developments since the Second Vatican Council.
Curiously, very little has been written about Religious Education in
that process of looking back in order to move forward. Yet it would
have to be admitted that in any general review of Church life since
the Second Vatican Council, Religious Education would have to figure
prominently.

In Ireland, there have been very significant developments in the short
span of twenty years. On the credit side, there has been the creation
of a very impressive programme of catechetical texts at the primary
and post-primary levels. Two new Institutes of Religious Education
came into existence: Mater Dei in Dublin and Mount Oliver in
Dundalk. These two Institutes have turned out over one thousand
trained catechists who have contributed quietly and unobtrusively to
the life and faith of the Catholic Church in Ireland. In addition, you

had the foundation of the Catechetical Association of Ireland which gave important direction and inspiration through weekend conferences to religion teachers up and down the country. Further, you had the creation of the quarterly journal, *The Irish Catechist*, which provided an important forum for the exchange of catechetical ideas. Lastly, you had the appointment by individual bishops of 'Diocesan Advisers' at primary and post-primary levels to support teachers of religion, as well as the setting up of Catechetical and Educational Commissions by the Irish Hierarchy to overview developments. These innovative steps taken in the late sixties and early seventies have served Religious Education constructively in Ireland over the last twenty years.

On the debit side, there has been the serious failure to link school, parish and home in the common task of Religious Education. Adult Religious Education as the primary form of religious Education is not yet fully appreciated, though considerable progress has been made in more recent years. A great need exists for in-service courses for religious educators who, once qualified, are all too often forgotten about and all too easily isolated, with no apparent support from the institutional Church. The development of a new christian philosophy of education is a particularly urgent task at this stage in Irish education. Lastly, a more open and trusting dialogue between civil authorities and Church bodies on areas of mutual interest in education needs to be developed.

In the area of general education there has been the publication of quite a few important documents in the last few years by Government agencies. Let me briefly refer to those which have some bearing on Religious Education. In 1983 you had the appearance of the *Programme for Action in Education* which talks quite explicitly about religious studies and Religious Education.[1] This document in turn was followed up by the publication of *Issues and Structures in Education* (1984) which gave generous recognition to religion under different headings: Religious Education, Comparative Religion, Religious Studies, and Moral Education. Thirdly, there was the document *Ages for Learning: Decisions of Government* (1985) and its follow-up *Transition Year Programmes* (1986) which in its own way poses searching questions for the development of Religious Education in a new context, an issue I will return to later. While these documents are primarily about developments in education in general, they do nonetheless, provide part of the context that should be taken into consideration in any analysis of the challenge facing Religious Education today.

Another aspect of the context that must be faced in any discussion

1.   See Response by Mater Dei Academic Staff to this document in *The Furrow*, October 1984, pp. 639-647.

about Religious Education concerns developments in theology. What goes on in theology does have implications for Religious Education. This does not mean that Religious Education is 'the messenger boy' of theology. It does mean, however, that shifts and new emphases in theology should be reflected in Religious Education. It would be a brave person who would claim to sum up developments in theology over the last twenty years. Yet, I think it is possible to discern some general shifts. Chief among these is the existence of political theology in Europe, liberation theology in Latin America, and more recently what is called practical theology in North America.[2] While these developments may appear to some as dangerous and to others as deviations to be avoided, I think there is sufficient evidence to suggest that the general direction they point us in, as distinct from some of the details, has become part and parcel of the mainstream of theology. Indeed, much of the language and outlook of these theologies has become part of the language and outlook of official Church statements, despite warnings about some excesses.[3] In addition, there is the growing body of social teaching by the Church over the last twenty years symbolised in documents like *On the Development of Peoples* by Paul VI, the 1971 Synodal document *Justice in the World*, and the Puebla *Conclusions* of the Latin American Bishops' Conference in 1979. These developments in the Church's social teaching are an important part of the context in which we must look at the challenge facing Religious Education today.

Another factor colouring the challenge facing Religious Education is the changed social and cultural atmosphere in which the teaching of religion must take place. In a sense, this is one of the most important and complex factors affecting Religious Education today. For that reason it is also the most difficult to sum up adequately. This new situation is often referred to in terms of secularization and the accompanying phenomena of individualism, consumerism, competitiveness, and religious indifference.

Perhaps a more helpful way of describing this situation is to talk about the emergence of a new kind of historical consciousness in this century. Today, more than ever before, we have become aware of

2.   See *Practical Theology* edited by D.S. Browning, San Francisco: Harper & Row, 1983.
3.   These warnings, especially the "Instruction on Certain Aspects of the 'Theology of Liberation'" put out by the Sacred Congregation for the Doctrine of the Faith in 1984 should be balanced by the positive and well-received "Instruction on Christian Freedom and Liberation" published by the same Congregation in 1986.

ourselves as historical subjects who are responsible for shaping our individual destinies in the world we inhabit. More and more we realize that it is human beings who have created the social and cultural structures that make up the fabric of life. We realize more than ever before that it is humanity who can change and transform these structures. The human race has become frighteningly aware of its freedom to accept the world as it is or to change the course of history. All the resources necessary to change the face of the earth are available: scientific, technological and political. Alternatively we can acquiesce in the unjust social structures of the world that surround us. What this means in effect is that there is very little that can be said to be divinely preordained about the world as we know it; there is nothing sacrosanct about the imbalances, the injustices and inequalities that exist in the world today and which threaten the future of our planet.

Another way of describing this state of affairs is to acknowledge that we have moved from a rather static and fixed perception of the world to a much more dynamic and open-ended view of history. Within this changed perception, we have come to a deeper awareness of the historicity of the whole of human existence, especially the historicity of the social and cultural structures of the world we inhabit. This new sense of historicity highlights the persistent presence of change in the world around us as well as the apparent autonomy of so many aspects of life. If we wish to call this secularization, and I believe that is close enough to the real meaning of secularization, then it should be clear that the phenomenon of secularization brings with it new opportunities and new responsibilities. These responsibilities, especially in terms of the kind of world we would like to live in, tax our human resources and creative imagination at a most fundamental level. To this extent it must be said that secularization is as much an opportunity and challenge to Religious Education as it is a threat.

This changed context in which Religious Education must take place has been summed up by Bernard Lonergan in terms of a fundamental shift away from classical culture to a modern historical-minded culture.[4] Classical culture was stable, normative and universal, dealing with what it called the unchanging essence of things. In contrast, our modern culture is mobile, relative and historical focusing on what can be changed in the present for the future.[5] According to classical culture, the world is naturally hierarchical, closed and enduring,

4. B. Lonergan, "The Transition from a Classicist World View to Historical Mindedness", *Second Collection*, W.J. Ryan and B.J. Tyrel (eds.), London: D.L.T., 1974, pp. 1-9.
5. B. Lonergan, "Belief: Today's Issue". *Second Collection*, pp. 91-93.

whereas modern culture sees the world as homogeneous, open-ended and unfinished. Whether this is a good thing or a bad thing is a matter of debate. The point to be noted is that we now live in a world which is quite different to the pre-enlightenment world of classical culture. This cultural shift was recognized by the Second Vatican Council in its *Constitution on the Church in the Modern World* and was seen as something that had serious "repercussions on man's religious life".[6]

A corollary to this distinctively modern mode of historical consciousness is the growing sense of the unity and solidarity of the human race. This can be seen in the different solidarity movements that have come into existence in recent times: from solidarity among workers to solidarity among peace people, to solidarity of, with and for the poor as well as solidarity of, with and for women. This thrust towards a new awareness of the fundamental solidarity of the human family is more than just a fashionable trend provoked by the mass media and the nuclear threat. The solidarity of all human beings seems to correspond to that which is fundamental to human identity and to survival. To ignore our solidarity with the past or to deny our solidarity in the present would be to cut ourselves off from the basic sources of life and survival. This new sense of solidarity seems to be constitutive of what it means to be human. It exists in marked contrast to the jaded individualism, the insensitive competitiveness and the excessive consumerism of the western world.

These different factors such as the above changes in Religious Education and education in general, developments in theology, the existence of social and cultural shifts, and the new sense of solidarity all have a direct bearing on the way we see the challenge facing Religious Education.

A General Description of the Challenge

How then are we to describe the challenge facing Religious Education in the light of these changes? In one sense, the challenge facing Religious Education is the same from one generation to the next. It is the task of communicating the experience of God to people. Religious Education, broadly speaking, is about enabling people to discover:

— that whether they know it or not, whether they reflect on it or not, they are always and everywhere directed and oriented to the transcendent mystery we call God,[7]

---

6. *Constitution on the Church in the Modern World*, a. 4.
7. This particular formulation is taken from K. Rahner in *K. Rahner : Im Gespräch*, Band I: 1964-1977. P. Imhof and H. Biallowons (eds.) Munich: Kosel, 1982, p. 301

— that the ultimate meaning of life is grounded in the living reality of God,
— that the world as we know it and experience it does have a divine purpose and final destiny.

It is important to stress here that this communication of the experience of God is not about the introduction of something new from the outside that is discontinuous, as it were, with the ordinary everyday experience. Instead, we should be clear from the outset that Religious Education is about making people aware of and sensitive to what is already going on in their lives. Religious Education is a process of explicating the co-presence of the religious dimension implicit in the whole of human experience.[8] Rahner gets it right when he says:

> The grace of God has always been there...ahead of our preaching (and teaching). . . Our preaching (and teaching) is not really an indoctrination with something alien from outside but the awakening of something within, as yet not understood but nevertheless really present.[9]

In addition to this foundational challenge there is also the specifically christian task of showing how the person of Christ lights up our experience of God and transforms our understanding of human existence. The gospel of Christ sharpens our awareness of the religious dimension of human experience. This specifically christian task facing Religious Education is described in different ways: handing on the faith, passing on the Good News, proclaiming the christian message, translating the christian tradition, sharing our faith story with others. . . Implicit here is the challenge of inserting the message of Christ into the contemporary situation without losing its unique identity. How does the saving gospel of Christ liberate people today in the twentieth century; how can christian faith interact with contemporary experience; can the Good News of the first century continue to be Good News in a world that is culturally quite different from the world of two thousand years ago?

For many people the problem with christianity has less to do with its message and more to do with the difference it makes or does not make to daily existence. Does the message of Christ make demands and if so, what kind of demands, or is the faith just a theoretical

8. The idea of the co-presence of God in human experience is developed in D. Lane, *The Experience of God,* Dublin, Veritas Publications, 1981, Cht 1.
9. K. Rahner, *Mission and Grace*, Vol. 1. London: Sheed & Ward, 1963, p. 156. The brackets have been added to this text.

construct that we adhere to in much the same way as we adhere to the rules of the golf club? Is christian faith a purely private affair or does it have public, social significance over and above going to Mass on Sundays? Is christianity simply a spiritual religion concerned exclusively with the world of supernatural realities or does it somehow touch the earthly and the natural side of life? Does it colour our choices and decisions and activities? Does faith involve taking sides in the struggle for justice in the world, in the concern for human rights, in the pursuit of the fundamental equality of all human beings?

These are hardly new questions. They were raised at Vatican II in terms of the gap that exists between life and religion, between experience and faith, between the gospel and culture which the Council called one of the most serious errors of the twentieth century.[10] Some might argue that this gap has been overcome to a large degree by Religious Education through its emphasis on the experiential and personal approaches to teaching.

My specific concern here goes beyond the experiential to practical questions about the social and political implications of christian faith today. Is it not true that the turn to experience that has been so prominent in Religious Education carries with it an equally important turn to social action? Must we not say that knowing the truth for the christian implies at the same time a radical responsibility for doing the truth? Does not the call to personal conversion include equally within it a commitment to social transformation? Is it not necessary just now in Religious Education to make more explicit the intrinsic connection between religious experience and social reconstruction?

It was these kinds of questions that prompted George Albert Coe, one of the great religious educators of North America, to ask in 1917:

> Shall the primary purpose of christian education be to hand on a religion, or to create a new world?[11]

In this stark question, Coe captures the precise terms of the contemporary challenge facing Religious Education. By formulating the question in this way, Coe was reacting against a view of Religious Education prevalent among some at that time, which saw it primarily in terms of handing down a closed system of dogmas and moral laws that had little or no bearing on the social, political and cultural world.

Coe's articulation of the question is as valid today as it was sixty-nine years ago. For Coe the primary purpose of Religious Education

10. *Constitution on the Church in the Modern World*, a. 43.
11. G.A. Coe, *What is Christian Education*, New York: C. Scribner's Sons, 1929, p.29.

is to change the world. The role of religion is to bring about a social reconstruction of the world. The reason for this, according to Coe, who was considerably influenced by Dewey, is that "reconstruction, continuous reconstruction, is of the essence of the divine work in and through the human."[12]

Some sixty years later, in 1978 to be exact, a symposium was held in Boston College to address Coe's question. Is Religious Education about handing on the faith or changing the world, is Religious Education about passing on the tradition or the transformation of society? The four main contributors to that symposium all agreed that Religious Education is about handing on the christian faith *and* transforming the world.[13]

In 1980 Tom Groome published an important work entitled *Christian Religious Education*.[14] Groome opts for what he calls "the shared praxis approach to Religious Education". He argues persuasively for the need to integrate theory and practice, faith and action, tradition and transformation. Yet, when it comes to outlining the five movements of the shared praxis approach, he does not specifically mention the importance of providing an experience of actually trying to change the world. My impression is, if I have understood Groome correctly, that the shared praxis which he impressively advocated does not go far enough. He stops short of including an experience of social action as something intrinsic to the process of religious education. The shared praxis that Groome talks about is one of comparing and contrasting 'my' story with the christian story and vision for the express purpose of bringing about conversion, decisions and choices. Of course, the conversion, decisions and choices imply and demand a new kind of action and performance in the life of the individual. All of this is implied in Groome's book. My unease, however, is that the follow-through of conversion, decisions and choices arising out of the christian story and vision is not sufficiently embraced as constitutive of the process of Religious Education. Clearly, it is implied in Groome but it is not found among the five movements describing the dynamics of shared praxis. As one observer noted, commenting on an article by Groome that preceded the publication of his book:

12. Ibid, 35.
13. See M. Boys, M. Harris, G.E. Nelson, and L.M Russell in P. O'Hare (ed.), *Tradition and Transformation in Religious Education*, Alabama: R.E.P., 1979.
14. T. Groome, *Christian Religious Education*, San Francisco: Harper and Row, 1980.

Shared praxis should include, if it is to be as fruitful as it can be, not only shared reflection but shared action.[15]

In 1983 an important collection of essays was put together by Padraig O'Hare entitled *Education for Justice and Peace*. A basic theme running through this collection is the claim that programmes of Religious Education should include opportunities for an experience of creating a more just world.[16]

Again, in 1983, the Religious Education Association of the U.S. took up the subject of 'Pursuing Justice and Peace' as the basic theme of its annual meeting. In preparation for the annual conference the *Journal of Religious Education* published a special issue devoted to the topic of 'Education for Social Responsibility'. In the lead article emphasis is placed on action for justice as something that should be built into the curriculum of Religious Education programmes.[17] This brief historical overview of the challenge facing Religious Education helps to focus on the issues. More and more there is a growing concern among religious educators for the integration of social justice issues into Religious Education programmes. This integration of action for justice within Religious Education must take place in the context of the christian tradition. The challenge, therefore, facing Religious Education today is twofold.

On the one hand, Religious Education must dialogue with the living tradition of christianity and at the same time become involved in the transformation of society. The danger and temptation facing Religious Education is to opt only for the second half of the challenge, namely the creation of a better world to the neglect of the first half of the challenge which is one of retrieving the christian tradition in a way that speaks to the contemporary situation. These two aspects of the challenge facing Religious Education today need to be kept together in creative tension. The transformation of the world requires the wisdom of the christian tradition and the wisdom of christian tradition must be seen to lead to the work of transforming the world. The recovery of the dynamism of the christian message will give rise to action for justice and the transformation of society will reawaken the vision of christian faith. In other words, the challenge facing Religious Education today is one of integrating tradition and transformation,

15. F. Darcy-Bérubé, "The Challenge Ahead of Us", *Foundations of Religious Education*, P. O'Hare (ed.) Paulist Press, 1978, p.127.
16. P. O'Hare (ed.) *Education for Justice and Peace*, San Francisco: Harper and Row, 1983, pp. 8, 10, 80, 155.
17. W. B. Kennedy, "Pursuing Justice and Peace: Challenge to Religious Education", *Religious Education*, Fall 1983, pp. 467-476 at 474.

bringing together the vision of christian faith with the demands of social activity, balancing the relationship between knowledge and christian action, embracing an understanding of faith with social reconstruction. Without this critical correlation between knowing and doing there is a real danger that our Religious Education will appear too theoretical, too idealistic and too cerebral. At the same time, however, unless the work of justice is inspired by the christian vision it will all too easily turn into one of the many 'isms' that are abroad: socialism, marxism, capitalism... For this reason, Religious Education must have some grasp of the liberating message it seeks to communicate as it gets involved in creative action for justice. Equally, however, if the faith that Religious Education communicates does not lead to action for justice, then there is a real possibility that its message may become a self-serving ideology. Clearly then, there are extremes to be avoided in the challenge presently facing Religious Education.

Analysis of the two sides of the challenge
In the light of this refinement of the challenge facing Religious Education let us now look more closely at what is involved in handing on the tradition. Here it must be pointed out that when we talk about tradition we are talking about a living tradition that embodies a vibrant faith and an active vision. We are not talking about some dead letter from the past, nor are we referring to what has come to be called 'traditionalism' which is concerned simply to repeat the past without taking account of the present. The point is sometimes made that the problem with 'traditionalism' is that it tends to represent 'the dead faith of the living' whereas tradition is about 'the living faith of the dead' that enlivens the christian community today.

Further, it must be noted that the christian tradition is not available to us as some kind of timeless truth or chemically pure essence or definable deposit. The Church has always recognized the fact that its message is contained in socially and culturally conditioned categories. Anyone with a sense of history will be aware of the presence of different cultural expressions of christian faith down through the ages. These vary from Jewish expressions of christian identity to Hellenistic statements of the meaning of christian faith to the presence of precise scholastic formulae in the middle ages, followed by Reformation and post-Reformation categories right into the emerging pluralism of the twentieth century. This point was made quite dramatically by Pope John XXIII at the opening of the Second Vatican Council when he pointed out that:

> The substance of the ancient doctrine of the deposit of faith is
> one thing, and the way it is expressed is another. And it is the

latter that must be taken into great consideration with patience if necessary...[18]

This distinction between the living tradition and its cultural expressions, between faith and its different historical forms, is important because the impression is often given that Religious Education is about handing down the faith in frozen forms and immutable categories. The 1980 Synod on Catechesis in its "Message to the People of God" cautioned against this kind of approach to Religious Education:

> Routine reiteration, with its refusal to accept any change; any improvisation with its readiness for any venture, are equally dangerous.[19]

Handing on the faith therefore does not bind us to the mere repetition of formulae belonging to another cultural era. Instead, passing on the tradition challenges each generation to find a language and framework in touch with contemporary experience which at the same time is faithful to the enduring message of Christ. If this challenge is neglected, then the message of Christ may be rejected for the wrong reasons.

In meeting this challenge Religious Education seeks to relate the living tradition of christianity to the experience of those it teaches. In doing so, Religious Education sets out to show how the christian tradition can throw light on the burning social and political questions facing humanity today. Likewise the christian tradition has a particular wisdom that can contribute to our contemporary understanding of human experience and the transformation of society.

At the same time this movement 'downwards' from tradition to experience must be enriched and complimented by an equally important movement 'upwards' from experience to tradition. It is this latter movement from experience to tradition that enables each generation to personalize and assimilate the living tradition. Each generation will do this by bringing its own particular needs and experiences to bear on the living tradition. It will do this in a positive way by recovering what was lost or perhaps forgotten in the tradition, for example in the way that Vatican II rediscovered the personal and historical and experiential aspects of revelation. Each generation will also react to the living tradition by refusing to accept whatever cultural distortions exist within the tradition, for example in the way that

18. "Pope John's Opening Speech to the Council", *The Documents of Vatican II*, N. Abbot (ed.) p. 715.
19. *L'Osservatore Romano*, October, 1977.

Vatican II came out explicitly against every form of discrimination whether racial, social or sexual.[20]

A two-way movement therefore must be allowed to take place in the process of handing on the living tradition of christianity. Tradition illuminates human experience and human experience challenges tradition. A creative interplay, a 'to-ing' and 'fro-ing' between tradition and experience must be allowed to take place within Religious Education. If the movement from experience to tradition is suppressed, then the message will become a dead letter or an empty formula to be handed down somewhat like a lifeless baton in a relay race. This is the danger with certain forms of 'traditionalism' as distinct from the dynamism of the living tradition.

If this delicate movement from tradition to experience *and* from experience to tradition is to succeed, and I don't underestimate the difficulties involved in this, then a visible line of continuity between the past and the present must become apparent. Part of the challenge facing Religious Education today is to keep that line of continuity both visible in the present and viable for the next generation.

In an era of great social and cultural upheaval, such as the present, it becomes all the more difficult to safeguard this principle of continuity. One way of doing this, recommended by the Second Vatican Council and repeated by the *General Catechetical Directory*, is to recognize the existence of a hierarchy of truths within the christian tradition.[21] Clearly, certain parts of the christian tradition are more central and more important than others. Some truths of the faith are foundational while others are derivative. Religious Education in a time of social and cultural transition must take account of the existence of the hierarchy of truths in handing on the christian tradition. Obviously, the communication of God as Father, Son and Spirit is more important in the process of Religious Education than the communication of idle speculations about limbo.

Having seen something about the dynamics involved in handing on the Christian tradition, I now want to turn to the other side of the challenge facing Religious Education namely that of changing the world. In making this transition from tradition to the transformation of society I would like to emphasise that we are dealing with something that can no longer be regarded as secondary or optional or merely additional to Religious Education. Instead, we are concerned with an aspect of Religious Education that is intrinsic to and constitutive of

20. *Constitution on the Church in the Modern world*, a. 29.
21. *Decree on Ecumenism*, a.11; *The General Catechetical Directory*, a. 43.

the living tradition we are passing on. The christian tradition we are handing down demands involvement in the transformation of the world.

In passing on the christian tradition, Religious Education aims:
— to awaken an experience and knowledge of God in its hearers,
— to foster a maturity of faith,
— to promote an explicit discipleship of Christ for the sake of the Kingdom of God.

A look at each of these three objectives will show that action for justice is something that is built into the christian tradition.

When we talk about awakening an experience of God we are not aiming to introduce people to some kind of exotic or unusual experience that is out of joint with their previous experiences of life. As already intimated, we are talking about people understanding in a new way what has already taken place in their experiences of existence. In talking about an experience of God, therefore, we are concerned to enable people to see what up to now they may not have seen fully, to hear what up to now they may not have been hearing fully. This point is well made by T.S. Eliot in the following lines:

> We shall not cease from exploration,
> And the end of our exploring,
> Will be to arrive where we started,
> And to know the place for the first time.[22]

Religious Education, therefore, is about enabling people to recognize explicitly the presence of God that is implicit in all human experience. This perception of the co-presence of God in human experience gives rise to a special kind of knowledge that is quite different from scientific knowledge or merely informational knowledge. The knowledge which accompanies an experience of God is knowledge in the biblical sense, i.e. a knowledge which originates in the heart combining understanding and loving, knowing and doing. According to the biblical tradition, to know God is to do the will of God, more specifically to experience God is to do justice. (*Jer 22 15-16; Mt 7:21; 1 Jn 4:7-8*). This experience and knowledge of God that Religious Education seeks to promote is something that leads the individual to a new kind of lifestyle, one that compels the individual to become involved in issues of justice and peace and reconciliation in our world. As one commentator points out:

> The experience of God catapults the person into the world with the divine agenda.[23]

22. T. S. Eliot, *Little Gidding*.
23. J. Shea, *An Experience Named Spirit*, Chicago: Thomas More Press, 1985, p. 73.

The knowledge of God, therefore, that Religious Education seeks to promote is that special kind of knowledge that is born out of the experience of the love of God flooding our hearts, an experience that calls for action for justice and solidarity with others.

This particular experience and knowledge of God is closely related to the maturity of faith that Religious Education seeks to foster. The faith in question is always a personal faith, being made up of a personal response and surrender to the love of God revealed in Christ. This deeply personal act of faith finds expression in the classical statements summarizing the content of faith. Personal faith, which is always free and can never be forced, depends on these classical formulae. These statements of faith are to be found in the biblical stories, the early creeds, the liturgical forms, and the moral principles of the christian tradition. Personal faith is sustained by these traditional statements of faith. Yet, and this point needs to be stressed, the personal act of faith can not be reduced to a series of classical statements, traditional formulae or contemporary catechetical texts. Without attention to the primacy of the personal dimension of the act of faith, and all the struggle and doubt and darkness that are a natural part of that act of faith, we run the risk of passing on 'the faith' without faith.

Further, within the context of this primacy of the personal dimension of the act of faith, major emphasis must be placed on the activities of trusting and loving and surrendering that go up to make that act of faith. It is only within the experience of responding and surrendering ourselves to God that the full meaning of faith is disclosed. Likewise it is only in the experience of venturing forth in love and trust that the higher levels of meaning that belong to faith fully emerge. In this sense, faith is an activity in the life of the individual: it is a way of acting and living in the world. Faith, therefore, is as much something we do as it is something we have. Without this important emphasis on activity and doing, faith is in danger of becoming something else. It is this particular focus on doing within faith that is to the fore in the New Testament: in the sayings of Jesus (*Mt 7:21; Mt 5:23-24; Mt 25:34-36*), in the writings of Paul (*1 Cor 4:20*) and John (*1 Jn 3:17-18; 1 Jn 4:7-8*), and above all in the epistle of James which discusses at length the emptiness of faith without good works (*James 2:1-26*). Further, this emphasis on faith has been recovered in a striking way by contemporary theology which highlights the performative aspects of christian faith.[24] The maturity of faith that Religious

24. See J. C. Haughey (ed.), *The Faith that Does Justice*, New York: Paulist Press, 1977, especially the article by A. Dulles, "The Meaning of Faith Considered in Relation to Justice", pp. 10-46.

Education seeks to promote is a faith that is active in its origins and finality.

The third goal of Religious Education which I mentioned is the promotion of discipleship of Christ for the sake of the kingdom of God. There are two key ideas here: discipleship of Christ and the reign of God. Discipleship, especially a discipleship of equals among equals, is at the centre of the gospel and this category seems to sum up better than most, what is involved in being a christian. Discipleship embraces a sense of calling, a need for conversion at the spiritual and social levels, and the adoption of a new lifestyle. Each of these dimensions of discipleship is coloured by the horizons of the reign of God. The kingdom of God as preached by Jesus is a vision about the possibility of a new order of existence in which the justice and peace and love of God takes over the minds and hearts of women and men in this life and in the future. This new order is not just a dream but is something that is brought into being when the blind see, the deaf hear, the lame walk, the sick are healed, and the dead are raised up (*Lk 7:18-22*). The disciples of Christ are called and commissioned to work for the new reign of God. The reign of God announced and realized by Christ introduces a new vision and commands a new action in our world. By focusing on discipleship and the kingdom of God, Religious Education once again discovers the practical and transformative implications of its goal.

This emphasis on the transformative demands of the gospel of Christ is something that was explicitly recovered at Vatican II. It has since moved to the centre of the christian stage. The major breakthrough came in the *Pastoral Constitution on the Church in the Modern World*. In that foundational document, an important dialogue was set in motion between the Church and the world, between faith and culture. This dialogue, especially in its implications, was taken up in post conciliar documents: from the 1967 Encyclical of Paul VI on *The Development of Peoples* to *Laborem Exercens* of John Paul II of 1981, from Medellin of 1968 to Puebla of 1979, from the 1969 Synod to the Extraordinary Synod of 1985. By far the most important statement of this dialogue between the Church and the world, between faith and culture, is to be found in the 1971 synodal document *Justice in the World*:

> Action for justice and participation in the transformation of the world appear to us as a constitutive dimension of the preaching of the gospel.[25]

25. *Justice in the World* "Introduction".

This statement brings out clearly and unabiguously the intrinsic connection between the gospel and the transformation of the world. Replace the word 'preaching' by 'teaching' and we get some idea of how urgent it is for Religious Education to incorporate the creative work of justice into its agenda.

Looking at the implications of the challenge
At this stage I want to examine some of the practical implications of this challenge facing Religious Education. Clearly it means first of all that the handing on of the faith must bring out the active, liberative and transformative developments of the message of Christ. However, to talk about action for justice without engaging in action for justice, to be concerned about changing the world without becoming involved in that process, to be in favour of liberating the oppressed without doing anything about it, is to shortchange the gospel of Christ and call into question the validity of our teaching. Consequently, a major implication of this challenge facing Religious Education is that the process of understanding faith must be complimented by an experience of faith grounded in action for justice. This latter activity in turn must become the data of further reflection within the community or classroom situation. Believing must be strengthened by witnessing, and witnessing must be informed by believing. A creative dialectic between theory and practice, between action and reflection, between knowing and doing, must become the hallmark of Religious Education in the future. Handing on the faith must be accompanied by a visible involvement in the transformation of society. Teaching the gospel of Christ must include a creative moment of living the gospel. Shared reflection on faith in groups must give rise to shared action by the group in the local community.

This does not mean topping up Religious Education programmes with a dash of action for justice here and there. Nor does it mean adopting a social service project as some kind of addendum to Religious Education. Nor does it mean playing down the reflective and interpretative aspects of Religious Education and upgrading fieldwork. To react in any one of these ways is to miss the radical character of what is being proposed. Likewise, it is to trivialize the work of justice to the level of just another gimmick for Religious Education.

Instead, what is being proposed here is the adoption of a new post-liberal philosophy of education for Religious Education. We are suggesting that the more traditional philosophy of education which emphasises learning for the sake of learning through the time-honoured process of understanding and reflection be supplemented. Without prejudice to the centrality of understanding we are proposing that part of the data for reflection should come from the actual experience of being involved in the creation of a better world. In this way, the important process of understanding and interpretation will take on a new sharpness and immediacy. Further, we are suggesting the adoption by Religious Education of that philosophy of knowing which combines a dialectical relationship between action and reflection, theory and practice, experience and understanding, fieldwork and interpretation.

A new pedagogical principle, therefore, is being proposed for Religious Education, not in opposition to the more traditional way of knowing but as a complement and a corrective. It is a pedagogical principle that could be traced back via Paolo Freire and others to Aristotle. There is a wisdom that comes through the crucible of shared action that enlightens the insights of reflection and contemplation. That wisdom which comes through the pain of failure and the joy of success in action for justice should become part of the process of Religious Education.

Traditionally we have come to know and understand by reflecting on the world as it is, assuming that knowledge is the outcome of some kind of correspondence and conformity of the mind to reality. The supposition behind this way of knowing is that the world as it is given is the world as it was intended by the creator. Likewise, it is assumed that the world as we know it is a closed and fixed system. These suppositions are not as self-evident as they were in the past. The world as we experience it today reflects traces of human beings as much as it does of its creator. Equally, the world is experienced more and more as an open, unfinished project rather than a closed, fixed system. In view of this ambiguity surrounding the world we live in today, there is the task facing humanity of assuming a greater degree of responsibility for shaping the future of our world. That global task must become part of the agenda facing Religious Education today. By taking on this responsibility and becoming involved in changing the world from the way it is to the way it might be, a new kind of knowledge and understanding is given to Religious Education. In other words, I am suggesting that the educational principles of learning by doing and knowing through action be incorporated into the educational foundations of Religious Education.

Echoes of this approach to Religious Education can be found in recent statements by the Catholic Church on education. For example, the document put out by the Congregation for Catholic Education on *The Catholic School* in 1978 states:

> The Catholic school is particularly sensitive to the call from every part of the world for a more just society...It does not stop short

at courageous teachings of the demands of justice...but tries to put these demands into practice in its own community.[26]

Similarly, the 1979 document produced at Puebla by the Latin American Bishops points out:

That evangelising education should turn pupils into active subjects not only of their own development, but also of a service dedicated to the development of the whole community.

That same section goes on to say

Catholic education must produce agents who will effect the permanent, organic change that...society needs.[27]

If this proposal about the challenge facing Religious Education and its implications can be implemented, then Religious Education should be able to adjust to the new situation outlined at the beginning of this paper. In the first place, the incorporation of shared action for justice into our Religious Education programmes will give the teaching of Religion in our schools a prophetic edge and value. It will do this at a time in Ireland when a considerable amount of soul-searching is taking place about the basis of the Church's involvement in education. Surely this shift towards shared action for justice must become part of any description of what is distinctive about Catholic education today. Is it claiming too much to suggest that one of the main reasons for the Church's involvement in education is to respond to the gospel call, to care for the poor, to promote justice and to contribute to the transformation of society? Are we not close here, in part at least, to the identity of Catholic education? Further, if this shift towards community action for justice could become part of Religious Education in our schools, then an important bridge between school catechesis and parish catechesis could be constructed. The obvious place for implementing shared programmes of action for justice would be the local parish community, local organisations and voluntary bodies. In this way new links between school and parish could be established to the benefit of both communities. This involvement of school and parish in the process of Religious Education may be essential to the future of Catholic education in Ireland.

A new opening in this direction for Religious Education seems to be built into the *Transition Year Programmes* published by the Curriculum and Examinations Board in 1986. The proposal of transition years between the Intermediate and Leaving certificates and after Leaving certificate envisages a programme of alternative education

---

26. *The Catholic School*, London: C.T.S. 1977, a.58. See also a. 62.
27. *Puebla : Evangelisation at Present and in the Future of Latin America*, Slough: St Paul Publications, 1980, Nos. 1030 and 1033 respectively.

that combines content with work-experience, learning through community projects. It is important that Religious Education should take its place within this new system of alternative education. By doing so, Religious Education should be able to make its own particular contribution, both constructive and critical, to this new development in Irish education.

A further advantage for Religious Education stemming from this shift towards action for justice would be the provision of a new community context for the celebration of liturgy. If liturgy is about life situations and the building of community then the struggle for justice, as the biblical tradition reminds us forcefully, is one of the most appropriate points of entry into liturgy. At the same time the celebration of the Eucharist would enable Religious Education to keep the struggle for justice moving in the direction of the coming reign of God.[28]

What has been said here about Religious Education in schools also applies to adult Religious Education in parishes. Parish programmes of Religious Education, if they are to be true to the outlines proposed here, must concern themselves with experiences of shared action for justice directed towards both the christian community itself and the wider community.

In the second place, by incorporating creative action for justice into its programme, Religious Education will be taking account of developments that have taken place in theology over the last twenty years. In this way, basic themes like the preferential option for the poor, the struggle for justice, the defence of human rights, the equality and dignity of all persons, the creation of a better world, and concern for the development of the whole person would become part and parcel of Religious Education. More specifically it would become clear that talk about God, Christ, the Church, the sacraments and grace would centre itself around these basic themes. Thirdly, by accepting this challenge, Religious Education would find itself interacting with those questions which arise from what I have called the distinctively modern mode of historical consciousness. If it is true that humanity has self-consciously moved to the centre of the stage, and if it is true that humanity is now consciously involved in the making, unmaking and remaking of history, then Religious Education must become part of that process. Already we have striking evidence of the contribution that christian faith can make and is making to some of the burning issues of our specifically modern consciousness. One thinks immediately of the epoch-making U.S. Bishops' Pastoral on *The*

28. On the link between social justice and Eucharist see D. Lane, *Foundations for a Social theology*, Dublin: Gill and Macmillan, 1984, Ch. 6.

Challenge of Peace (1983) and their current reflections on *Catholic Social Teaching in the U.S. Economy*.[29] These responses to the signs of the times and their practical implications must become part of the agenda of Religious Education for tomorrow. As the world assumes more and more responsibility for its future, as human subjects begin to shape their own destinies, Religious Education must show how christian faith and its liberating activities do have a bearing on the future of humanity.

Fourthly, the growing sense of solidarity within the human family and the new awareness of our unity with creation cannot be ignored by Religious Education. By critically uniting knowing and doing, tradition and transformation, Religious Education will be serving that sense of solidarity and unity that belongs to humankind. In particular, Religious Education will be able to show through its involvement in action for justice that the ultimate source of solidarity is humanity's origin and destiny in God.

Finally and by way of conclusion, let me say that the challenge I have been describing for Religious Education will only succeed to the extent that a critical unity between theory and practice, action and reflection is maintained. Once the struggle for justice is separated from the christian vision, then Religious Education loses its particular identity and becomes reduced to the level of another social science. It cannot be over-emphasised, and we must continually remind ourselves, that Religious Education is about sharing a particular way of seeing, inducing a particular way of knowing, promoting a particular way of doing. It is, in the end, about communicating a vision of life that has been disclosed to us in the life, death and resurrection of Jesus. Without this vision, our creative activities are in danger of becoming mechanical methods and mere techniques giving us the illusion that we can free ourselves and change the world without reference to the transcendent source of salvation. This danger of severing action from the vision is summed up poignantly in the biblical story of Moses and Aaron. It is Moses who has been graced with the vision of Yahweh and given the Word of God; Aaron has the task of communicating this vision to the people and implementing it in life. All goes well as long as Moses with the vision and Aaron with the task stay together. When they become separated, when Aaron in the valley loses contact with Moses on the mountain with the vision, then you have the creation of the golden calf and all that goes with it. This story of Moses and Aaron is a stark reminder to us of how important it is for Religious Education to keep its vision and action together in meeting the challenge it must face in the years ahead.

29. See second draft "Catholic Social Teaching of the U.S. Economy", *Origins*, 10 October, 1985.

CONTRIBUTORS

Andreas Baur, Monsignor. Director of the Education Secretariate in the diocese of Augsburg, Professor of Religious Education and author of several books for primary and post-primary schools in Germany.

Didier Jacques Piveteau, F.S.C., Brother. Taught Catechetics at L'Institute Catholique, Paris, in Louvain, Belgium and at several centres in the U.S.A. for fifteen summers. Co-author of *The Resurgence of Religious Instruction*. Sadly, Brother Didier passed away on the 5th May, 1986. May he rest in peace.

Michael J. Wrenn, Monsignor. Founding Director of the Pontifical Archdiocesan Catechetical Institute of St. Joseph's Seminary, Dunwoodie, New York, which offers a Master's degree Programme in Religious Studies. Editor of Commentaries on *Catechesi Tradendi* and *Familiaris Consortio*.

Berard L. Marthaler, O.F.M.Conv. Professor of Religion and Religious Education at Catholic University of America, Washington D.C. Editor of *The Living Light: An Interdisciplinary Review* and author of recently published commentary on *The Creed* (XXIII Publications).

Michael Warren, Dr., Professor for Catechetical Ministry in the Department of Theology at St. John's University, New York. Editor of *Source Book for Modern Catechetics* and author of *Youth and the Future of the Church*.

Gabriel Moran, Dr., Professor of Religious Education at New York University, New York. Author of many articles and books, including *Religious Education Development*.

Una O'Neill, Sr., Member of Religious Sisters of Charity. Lecturer in Mater Dei Institute of Education and Superior of the community at St. Mary's Hospital, Baldoyle, Co. Dublin.

Donal Murray, Most Reverend. Auxiliary Bishop of Dublin. Formerly lecturer in Moral Theology at Mater Dei Institute. Member of the Secretariate for Non-Believers, Rome. Author of several publications including *The Future of the Faith*.

Kevin Nichols, Monsignor. Parish Priest of St. Mary's, Barnard Castle, Durham, England. Formerly National Adviser to the Bishops of England and Wales on Catechetics. Author of several books including *Cornerstone: Guidelines for Religious Education*.

Dermot A. Lane, Rev., Director of Studies at Mater Dei Institute of Education and lecturer in Theology at Clonliffe College. Author of *Foundations for a Social Theology*.

Index

Index

169

171

172